Appendix A

Appendix A:

Trust Resources and Other Species and Habitats of Special Management Concern

Codes used in Species Lists

Global Rank (from the Nature Conservancy)

G1 - Extremely rare and critically imperiled with 5 or fewer occurrences or very few remaining individuals;
or because of some factor(s) making it especially vulnerable to extinction.

G2 - Very rare and imperiled with 6 to 20 occurrences or few remaining individuals; or because of some factor(s) making it vulnerable to extinction.

G3 - Either very rare and local throughout its range or found locally (even abundantly at some of its locations) in a restricted range; or vulnerable to extinction because of other factors. Usually fewer than 100 occurrences are documented.

G4 - Common and apparently secure globally, though it may be rare in parts of its range, especially at the periphery.

G5 - Very common and demonstrably secure globally, though it may be rare in parts of its range, especially at the periphery.

GH - Formerly part of the world's fauna with some expectation that it may be rediscovered; generally applies to species that have not been verified for an extended period (usually >15 years) and for which some inventory has been attempted recently.

GX - Believed to be extinct throughout its range with virtually no likelihood of rediscovery.

GU - Possibly rare, but status uncertain and more data needed.

G? - Unranked, or, if following a ranking, rank uncertain (e.g., G3?).

G_G_ - The rank is uncertain, but considered to be within the indicated range of ranks (also, T_T_).

G_Q - Taxon has a questionable taxonomic assignment (e.g., G3Q).

G_T_ - Signifies the rank of a subspecies (e.g., G5T1 would apply to a subspecies if the species is demonstrably secure globally (G5) but the subspecies warrants a rank of T1, critically imperiled.)

State Rank

S1 - Extremely rare and critically imperiled with 5 or fewer occurrences or very few remaining individuals in Virginia; or because of some factor(s) making it especially vulnerable to extirpation in Virginia.

S2 - Very rare and imperiled with 6 to 20 occurrences or few remaining individuals in Virginia; or because of some factor(s) making it vulnerable to extirpation in Virginia.

S3 - Rare to uncommon in Virginia with between 20 and 100 occurrences; may have fewer occurrences if found to be common or abundant at some of these locations; may be somewhat vulnerable to extirpation in Virginia.

SH - Formerly part of Virginia's fauna with some expectation that it may be rediscovered; generally applies to species that have not been verified in the state for an extended period (usually >15 years) and for which some inventory has been attempted recently.

SX - Believed to be extirpated from Virginia with virtually no likelihood of rediscovery.

SR - Reported for Virginia, but without persuasive documentation that would provide a basis for either accepting or rejecting the report.

SU - Possibly rare, but status uncertain and more data needed.

S_? - Rank uncertain. For example the rank S2? denotes a species that may range from S1 to S3.

S_S_ - Rank is uncertain, but considered to be within the indicated range of ranks.

S_B/S_N - Breeding and nonbreeding status of an animal (primarily used for birds) in Virginia, when they differ.

SZN - Long distance migrant whose occurrences outside of the breeding season are not monitored or a species whose wintering populations are transitory and usually do not occur regularly at specific localities.

SN? - Long distance migrant that has been recorded north and south of Virginia waters and should eventually be found along the coast of Virginia.

SA - State accidental; not a regular member of the Virginia fauna but recorded in the state at least once.

Federal Status

LE - Listed Endangered. A taxon threatened with extinction throughout all or a significant portion of its range.

LT - Listed Threatened. A taxon likely to become endangered in the foreseeable future.

LT/SA - Listed as Threatened due to Similarity of Appearance. The species so closely resembles an endangered or threatened species or population that enforcement personnel of the U.S. Fish and Wildlife Service cannot readily distinguish between the taxa (e.g., the northern population of the bog turtle is federally listed as endangered, but turtles from the southern population, which includes Virginia, are not readily distinguishable from them).

LT/PDL - Listed as Threatened but proposed for delisting. The U.S. Fish and Wildlife Service has proposed that this species be removed from the list of Endangered and Threatened wildlife. However, at the present time, the species is still listed as Threatened pending further action and is thus protected under the Endangered Species Act.

PE - Proposed Endangered. A taxon proposed for listing as endangered.

PT - Proposed Threatened. A taxon proposed for listing as threatened.

C - Candidate. There is enough available information to propose the species for listing, but listing is "precluded by other pending proposals of higher priority". (Formerly Candidate, Category 1)

State Status

LE - Listed Endangered; defined as a species that is in danger of extinction throughout all or a significant portion of its range.

LT - Listed Threatened; defined as a species that is likely to become endangered within the foreseeable future.

SC - Special Concern; animals that merit special concern according to the Virginia Department of Game and Inland Fisheries. This is not a legal category.

Scientific Name	Common Name	Global Rank	State Rank	Federal Status	State Status
RARE PLANTS (Townsend 2001)					
Amaranthus pumilus Raf.	Seabeach amaranth	G2	SH	LT	
Chamaesyce bombensis (Jacq.) Dugand = *Euphobia ammanioides Kunth*	Southern sea sponge	G4G5	S2		
Paspalum distichum L.	Joint paspalum	G5	S1		
*Physalis walter*i Nutt	Dune ground-cherry	G4	S2		
Rhynchospora colorata (L.) H. Pfieffer	White-topped sedge	G5	S1		
Plant species on the State's Division of Natural Heritage's watch list					
Aristida tuberculosa Nutt.	Seabeach needlegrass	G5	S3		
Bacopa monnieri (L.) Pennell	Coastal water-hyssop	G5?	S3		
Ilex vomitoria Ait.	Yaupon holly	G5	S3		
Lechea maritima Leggett *ex* B.S.P. var. *virginica* Hodgon	Virginia beach pinweed	G5T3Q	S3		
Leptochloa fascicularis (Lam.) Gray var. *maritima* (Bickn.) Gleason	Long-awned sprangletop	G5T3T4	S3		
Oenothera oakesiana (Gray) J.W. Robbins *ex* S. Wats. & Coult.	Evening primrose	G4G5Q	SU		
Polygonella articulata (L.) Meisn.	Eastern jointwood	G5	S3		
Sesuvium maritimum (Walt.) B.S.P.	Sea-purslane	G5	S3		
Suaeda linearis (Ell.) Moq.	Tall sea blite	G5	S3		
Uniola paniculata L.	Sea oats	G5	S3		
Zanthoxylum clava-herculis L.	Southern prickly-ash	G5	S3		
RARE ANIMALS (Roble 2001)					
FISH					
Acipenser oxyrhynchus	Atlantic sturgeon	G3	S2	SC	
REPTILES					
Caretta caretta	Loggerhead sea turtle	G3	SIB, S1N	LT	LT
Lepidochelys kempii	Kemp's Ridley sea turtle	G1	S1N	LE	LE

Scientific Name	Common Name	Global Rank	State Rank	Federal Status	State Status
BIRDS					
Accipiter cooperii	Cooper's hawk	G5	S2B/S3N		
Actitis maculara	Spotted sandpiper	G5	S2B/SZN		
Aegolius acadicus	Northern saw-whet owl	G5	S1B/S1N		SC
Ammodramus caudacutus	Saltmarsh sharp-tailed sparrow	G4	S2B/S3N		SC
Ammodramus henslowii	Henslow's sparrow	G4	S1B		LT
Anas discors	Blue-winged teal	G5	S1B/S2N		
Anas strepera	Gadwall	G5	S2B/S3N		
Aquila chrysaetos	Golden eagle	G5	SHB/S1N		
Ardea alba	Great egret	G5	S2B/S3N		SC
Asio flammeus	Short-eared owl	G5	S1B/S3N		
Asio otus	Long-eared owl	G5	S1		SC
Bartramia longicauda	Upland sandpiper	G5	S1B/SZN		LT
Botaurus lentiginosus	American bittern	G4	S1B/S2N		
Carpodacus purpureus	Purple finch	G5	S1B/S5N		SC
Catharus guttatus	Hermit thrush	G5	S1B/S5N		SC
Catharus ustulatus	Swainson's thrush	G5	S1B/SZN		
Certhia americana	Brown creeper	G5	S2S3B/S5N		SC
Charadrius melodus	Piping plover	G3	S2B/S1N	LT	LT
Charadrius wilsonia	Wilson's plover	G5	S1B/SZN		LE
Chondestes grammacus	Lark sparrow	G5	SHB/SZN		
Circus cyaneus	Northern harrier	G5	S1S2B/S2S4N		SC
Cistothorus platensis	Sedge wren	G5	S1B/S1S2N		SC
Contopus borealis	Olive-sided flycatcher	G4	SHB/SZN		
Dendroica fusca	Blackburnian warbler	G5	S2B/SZN		
Dendroica magnolia	Magnolia warbler	G5	S2B/SZN		SC
Dolichonyx oryzivorus	Bobolink	G5	S1B/SZN		
Egretta caerulea	Little blue heron	G5	S2B/S3N		SC

Scientific Name	Common Name	Global Rank	State Rank	Federal Status	State Status
Egretta thula	Snowy egret	G5			
Egretta tricolor	Tricolored heron	G5	S2B/S3N		SC
Empidonax alnorum	Alder flycatcher	G5	S1B/SZN		SC
Empidonax flaviventris	Yellow-bellied flycatcher	G5	S1B/SZN		SC
Eudocimus albus	White ibis	G5	S1B/SAN		
Falco peregrinus	Peregrine falcon	G4	S1B/S2N		LE
Fulica americana	American coot	G5	S1BS5N		
Gallinula chloropus	Common moorhen	G5	S1B/S1N		SC
Haliaeetus leucocephalus	Bald eagle	G4	S2B/S3N	LT/PDL	LE
Himantopus mexicanus	Black-necked stilt	G5	S1B		
Ictinia mississippiensis	Mississippi kite	G5	S1B		
Ixobrychus exilis	Least bittern	G5	S2S3B/S3N		
Lanius ludovicianus	Loggerhead shrike	G4	S2B/S3N		LT
Laterallus jamaicensis	Black rail	G4	S2B/S2N		
Limnothlypis swainsonii	Swainson's warbler	G4	S2B/SZN		SC
Loxia curvirostra	Red crossbill	G5	S1B/SZN		SC
Melospiza georgiana	Swamp sparrow	G5	S1B/S4S5N		
Mergus merganser	Common merganser	G5	S1B/S4N		
Nyctanassa violocea = Nycticorax violaceus	Yellow-crowned night-heron	G5	S2B/S3N		SC
Nycticorax nycticorax	Black-crowned night-heron	G5	S2S3B/S4N		
Oporonis philadelphia	Mourning warbler	G5	S1B/SZN		SC
Pelecanus occidentalis	Brown pelican	G4	S1B/S3N		SC
Phalacrocorax auritus	Double-crested comorant	G5	S1B/S4N		
Plegadis falcinellus	Glossy ibis	G5	S2B/S1N		SC
Podilymbus podiceps	Pied-billed grebe	G5	S2B/S3N		
Porzana carolina	Sora	G5	S1B/S2N		
Rallus elegans	King rail	G4G5	S2B/S3B		
Rallus limicola	Virginia rail	G5	S2B/S3N		

Scientific Name	Common Name	Global Rank	State Rank	Federal Status	State Status
Regulus satrapa	Golden-crowned kinglet	G5	S2B/S5N		SC
Rynchops niger	Black skimmer	G5	S2B/S1N		
Sitta canadensis	Red-breasted nuthatch	G5	S2B/S4N		SC
Sphyrapicus varius	Yellow-bellied sapsucker	G5	S1B/S4N		
Sterna antillarum	Least tern	G4	S2B/SZN		SC
Sterna caspia	Caspian tern	G5	S1B/S2N		SC
Sterna maxima	Royal tern	G5	S2B/SZN		
Sterna nilotica	Gull-billed tern	G5	S2B/SZN		LT
Sterna sandivicensis	Sandwich tern	G5	S1B/SZN		SC
Troglodytes troglodytes	Winter wren	G5	S2B/S4N		SC
Vermivora ruficapilla	Nashville warbler	G5	S1B/SZN		
MAMMALS					
Sylvilagus floridanus hitchnsi	Smith Island cottontail	G5THQ	SH		
ODONATA (Dragonflies & Damselflies)					
Anax longipes	Comet darner	G5	S2S3		
Celithemis verna	Double-ringed pennant	G5	S2S3		
Cordulegaster diastatops	Delta-spotted spiketail	G5	S1		
Enallagma dubium	Burgundy bluet	G5	S2		
Nannothemis bella	Elfin skimmer	G4	S1		
Nehalennia gracilis	Sphagnum sprite	G5	S2		
Nehalennia intergricollis	Southern sprite	G5	S2		
Somatochlora filosa	Fine-lined emerald	G5	S2		
Somatochlora provocans	Treetop emerald	G4	S2		
Sympetrum janae	Jane's meadowhawk	G5	SH		
COLEOPTERA (Beetles)					
Cicindela dorsalis dorsalis	Northern beach tiger beetle	G4T2	S2	LT	
Cicindela trifasciata	Tiger beetle	G5	S1		

Scientific Name	Common Name	Global Rank	State Rank	Federal Status	State Status
HETEROPTERA					
Bothynotus johnstoni	Mirid bug		G3	S1S3	
Botocudo modestus	Seed bug	G5	S1S3		
Pycnoderiella virginiana	Seashore plant bug	GU	SU		
Ploiaria carolina	Carolina thread-legged bug	G4?	S1S3		
Ploiaria hirticornis	Assassin bug	G3?	S1S3		
Pnirontis brimleyi	Assassin bug	G2	S1S3		
Ramphocorixa acuminata	Acuminate water boatman	G4	S1		
Ranatra drakei	Drake's water scorpion	G4	S1S3		
LEPIDOPTERA					
Butterflies and skippers:					
Caliphelis virginiensis	Little metalmark	G4	S1S2		
Callophrys irus	Frosted elfin	G3	S1		
Lycaena hyllus	Bronze copper	G5	S1		
Megathymus yuccae	Yucca giant skipper	G4	SH		
Moths:					
Drasteria graphica atlantica	Atlantic graphic moth	G4T4	S1S3		
Faronta rubripennis	Pink-streak moth	G3G4	S1S3		
Meropleon cosmion	A noctuid moth	G4	S1S3		
Papaipema araliae	Aralia shoot borer moth	G3G4	S2S3		
Papaipema duovata	Seaside goldenrod borer moth	G4	S1S3		
Papaipema stenocelis	Chain fern borer moth	G4	S1S3		
Papaipema speciosissima	Osmunda stern borer moth	G4	S1S3		
Schinia siren	Flower moth	G?	S1S2		

Appendix B:

Relevant Federal Laws

Relevant Federal Laws

This Act authorized the purchase of wetlands from Land and Water Conservation Fund moneys, removing a prior prohibition on such acquisitions. The Act also requires the Secretary to establish a National Wetlands Priority Conservation Plan, requires the States to include wetlands in their Comprehensive Outdoor Recreation Plans, and transfers to the Migratory Bird Conservation Fund amount equal to import duties on arms and ammunition.

Endangered Species Act of 1973 (16 U.S.C. 1531-1544, 87 Stat. 884), as amended

Public Law 93-205, approved December 28, 1973, repealed the Endangered Species Conservation Act of December 5, 1969 (P.L. 91-135, 83 Stat. 275). The 1969 act had amended the Endangered Species Preservation Act of October 15, 1966 (P.L. 89-669, 80 Stat. 926).
The 1973 Endangered Species Act provided for the conservation of ecosystems upon which threatened and endangered species of fish, wildlife, and plants depend, both through Federal action and by encouraging the establishment of State programs. The Act:

- Authorizes the determination and listing of species as endangered and threatened;

- Prohibits unauthorized taking, possession, sale, and transport of endangered species;

- Provides authority to acquire land for the conservation of listed species, using land and water conservation funds;

- Authorizes establishment of cooperative agreements and grants-in-aid to States that establish and maintain active and adequate programs for endangered and threatened wildlife and plants;

- Authorizes the assessment of civil and criminal penalties for violating the Act or regulations; and

- Authorizes the payment of rewards to anyone furnishing information leading to arrest and conviction for any violation of the Act of any regulation issued thereunder.

Environmental Education Act of 1990 (20 USC 5501-5510; 104 Stat. 3325)

Public Law 101-619, signed November 16, 1990, established the Office of Environmental Education within the Environmental Protection Agency to develop and administer a Federal environ. education program.

Responsibilities of the Office include developing and supporting programs to improve understanding of the natural and developed environment, and the relationships between humans and their environment; supporting the dissemination of educational materials; developing and supporting training programs and environmental education seminars; managing a Federal grant program; and administering an environmental internship and fellowship program. The Office is required to develop and support environmental programs in consultation with other Federal natural resource management agencies, including the Fish and Wildlife Service.

Executive Order 11988, Floodplain Management

The purpose of this Executive Order, signed May 24, 1977, is to prevent Federal agencies from contributing to the "adverse impacts associated with occupancy and modification of floodplains" and the "directt or indirect support of floodplain development." In the course of fulfilling their respective authorities,

Federal agencies "shall take action to reduce the risk of flood loss, to minimize the impact of floods on human safety, health and welfare, and to restore and preserve the natural and beneficial values served by floodplains.

Fish and Wildlife Improvement Act of 1978

This act was passed to improve the administration of fish and wildlife programs and amends amends several earlier laws, including the Refuge Recreation Act, the National Wildlife Refuge Administration Act, and the Fish and Wildlife Act of 1956. It authorizes the Secretary to accept gifts and bequests of real and personal property on behalf of the United States. It also authorizes the use of volunteers on Service projects and appropriations to carry out volunteer programs.

Historic Preservation Acts

There are various laws for the preservation of historic sites and objects.

Antiquities Act (16 USC 431 - 433) – The Act of June 8, 1906, (34 Stat. 225) authorizes the President to designate as National Monuments objects or areas of historic or scientific interest on lands owned or controlled by the United States. The Act required that a permit be obtained for examination of ruins, excavation of archaeological sites and the gathering of objects of antiquity on lands under the jurisdiction of the Secretaries of Interior, Agriculture, and Army, and provided penalties for violations.

Archaeological Resources Protection Act (16 U.S.C. 470aa - 470ll) -- Public Law 96-95, approved October 31, 1979, (93 Stat. 721) largely supplanted the resource protection provisions of the Antiquities Act for archaeological items.

This Act established detailed requirements for issuance of permits for any excavation for or removal of archaeological resources from Federal or Indian lands. It also established civil and criminal penalties for the unauthorized excavation, removal, or damage of any such resources; for any trafficking in such resources removed from Federal or Indian land in violation of any provision of Federal law; and for interstate and foreign commerce in such resources acquired, transported or received in violation of any State or local law.

Public Law 100-588, approved November 3, 1988, (102 Stat. 2983) lowered the threshold value of artifacts triggering the felony provisions of the Act from $5,000 to $500, made attempting to commit an action prohibited by the Act a violation, and required the land managing agencies to establish public awareness programs regarding the value of archaeological resources to the Nation.

Archeological and Historic Preservation Act (16 USC 469-469c) -- Public Law 86-523, approved June 27, 1960, (74 Stat. 220) as amended by Public Law 93-291, approved May 24, 1974, (88 Stat. 174) to carry out the policy established by the Historic Sites Act (see below), directed Federal agencies to notify the Secretary of the Interior whenever they find a Federal or Federally assisted, licensed or permitted project may cause loss or destruction of significant scientific, prehistoric or archaeologic data. The Act authorized use of appropriated, donated and/or transferred funds for the recovery, protection and preservation of such data.

Historic Sites, Buildings and Antiquities Act (16 USC 461-462, 464-467) -- The Act of August 21, 1935, (49 Stat. 666) popularly known as the Historic Sites Act, as amended by Public Law 89-249, approved October 9, 1965, (79 Stat. 971) declared it a national policy to preserve historic sites and objects of national significance, including those located on refuges. It provided procedures for designation, acquisition, administration and protection of such sites. Among other things, National Historic and Natural Landmarks are designated under authority of this Act. As of January, 1989, 31 national wildlife refuges contained such sites.

National Historic Preservation Act of 1966 (16 U.S.C. 470-470b, 470c-470n) -- Public Law 89-665, approved October 15, 1966, (80 Stat. 915) and repeatedly amended, provided for preservation of significant historical features (buildings, objects and sites) through a grant-in-aid program to the States. It established a National Register of Historic Places and a program of matching grants under the existing National Trust for Historic Preservation (16 U.S.C. 468-468d).

The Act established an Advisory Council on Historic Preservation, which was made a permanent independent agency in Public Law 94-422, approved September 28, 1976 (90 Stat. 1319). That Act also created the Historic Preservation Fund. Federal agencies are directed to take into account the effects of their actions on items or sites listed or eligible for listing in the National Register.

As of January, 1989, 91 historic sites on national wildlife refuges have been placed on the National Register.

Land and Water Conservation Fund Act of 1948

This act provides funding through receipts from the sale of surplus federal land, appropriations from oil and gas receipts from the outer continental shelf, and other sources of for land acquisition under several authorities. Appropriations from the fund may be used for matching grants to states for outdoor recreation projects and for land acquisition by various federal agencies, including the Fish and Wildlife Service.

Migratory Bird Conservation Act of 1929 (16 U.S.C. 715-715d, 715e, 715f-715r)

This Act established the Migratory Bird Conservation Commission which consists of the Secretaries of the Interior (chairman), Agriculture, and Transportation, two members from the House of Representatives, and an ex-officio member from the state in which a project is located. The Commission approves acquisition of land and water, or interests therein, and sets the priorities for acquisition of lands by the Secretary for sanctuaries or for other management purposes. Under this Act, to acquire lands, or interests therein, the state concerned must consent to such acquisition by legislation. Such legislation has been enacted by most states.

Migratory Bird Hunting and Conservation Stamp Act (16 U.S.C. 718-718j, 48 Stat. 452), as amended

The "Duck Stamp Act," as this March 16, 1934, authority is commonly called, requires each waterfowl hunter 16 years of age or older to possess a valid Federal hunting stamp. Receipts from the sale of the stamp are deposited in a special Treasury account known as the Migratory Bird Conservation Fund and are not subject to appropriations.

National and Community Service Act of 1990 (42 USC 12401; 104 Stat. 3127)

Public Law 101-610, signed November 16, 1990, authorizes several programs to engage citizens of the U.S. in full- and/or part-time projects designed to combat illiteracy and poverty, provide job skills, enhance educational skills, and fulfill environmental needs. Several provisions are of particular interest to the U.S. Fish and Wildlife Service.

American Conservation and Youth Service Corps -- As a Federal grant program established under Subtitle C of the law, the Corps offers an opportunity for young adults between the ages of 16-25, or in the case of summer programs, 15-21, to engage in approved human and natural resources projects which benefit the public or are carried out on Federal or Indian lands.

To be eligible for assistance, natural resources programs will focus on improvement of wildlife habitat and recreational areas, fish culture, fishery assistance, erosion, wetlands protection, pollution control and similar projects. A stipend of not more than 100 percent of the poverty level will be paid to participants. A Commission established to administer the Youth Service Corps will make grants to States, the Secretaries of Agriculture and Interior and the Director of ACTION to carry out these responsibilities.

National and Community Service Act -- Will make grants to States for the creation of full-time and/or part-time programs for citizens over 17 years of age. Programs must be designed to fill unmet educational, human, environmental, and public safety needs. Initially, participants will receive post-employment benefits of up to $1000 per year for part-time and $2500 for full-time participants.

Thousand Points of Light -- Creates a non-profit Points of Light Foundation to administer programs to encourage citizens and institutions to volunteer in order to solve critical social issues, and to discover new leaders and develop institutions committed to serving others.

National Environmental Policy Act of 1969 (P.L. 91-190, 42 U.S.C. 4321-4347, January 1, 1970, 83 Stat. 852) as amended by P.L. 94-52, July 3, 1975, 89 Stat. 258, and P.L. 94-83, August 9, 1975, 89 Stat. 424)

Title I of the 1969 National Environmental Policy Act (NEPA) requires that all Federal agencies prepare detailed environmental impact statements for "every recommendation or report on proposals for legislation and other major Federal actions significantly affecting the quality of the human environment."

The 1969 statute stipulated the factors to be considered in environmental impact statements, and required that Federal agencies employ an interdisciplinary approach in related decision-making and develop means to ensure that unquantified environmental values are given appropriate consideration, along with economic and technical considerations.

Title II of this statute requires annual reports on environmental quality from the President to the Congress, and established a Council on Environmental Quality in the Executive Office of the President with specific duties and functions.

National Wildlife Refuge System Administration Act of 1966 (16 U.S.C. 668dd-668ee) as amended

This Act defines the National Wildlife Refuge System as including wildlife refuges, areas for protection and conservation of fish and wildlife which are threatened with extinction, wildlife ranges, game ranges, wildlife management areas, and waterfowl production areas. The Secretary is authorized to permit any use of an area provided such use is compatible with the major purposes for which such area was established. The purchase consideration for rights-of-way go into the Migratory Bird Conservation Fund for the acquisition of lands. By regulation, up to 40% of an area acquired for a migratory bird sanctuary may be opened to migratory bird hunting unless the Secretary finds that the taking of any species of migratory game birds in more than 40% of such area would be beneficial to the species. The Act requires an Act of Congress for the divestiture of lands in the system, except (1) lands acquired with Migratory Bird Conservation Commission funds, and (2) lands can be removed from the system by land exchange, or if brought into the system by a cooperative agreement, then pursuant to the terms of the agreement.

National Wildlife Refuge System Centennial Act of 2000

The National Wildlife Refuge System Centennial Act of 2000 paves the way for a special, nationwide outreach campaign. The law calls for a Centennial Commission of distinguished individuals to leverage with partners in carrying out the outreach campaign. The law also calls for a long-term plan to address the major operations, maintenance, and construction needs of the National Wildlife Refuge System. These Centennial activities will help broaden visibility, strengthen partnerships, and fortify facilities and programs for wildlife and habitat conservation and recreation. They will build a stronghold of support for the National Wildlife Refuge System to sustain it in a new era of both challenge and opportunity.

National Wildlife Refuge System Improvement Act of 1997

Public Law 105-57, amends the National Wildlife System Act of 1966 (16 U.S.C. 668dd-ee), providing guidance for management and public use of the Refuge System. The Act mandates that the Refuge System be consistently directed and managed as a national system of lands and waters devoted to wildlife conservation and management.

The Act establishes priorities for recreational uses of the Refuge System. Six wildlife-dependent uses are specifically named in the Act: hunting, fishing, wildlife observation and photography, and environmental education and interpretation. These activities are to be promoted on the Refuge System, while all non-wildlife dependant uses are subject to compatibility determinations.

A compatible use is one which, in the sound professional judgement of the Refuge Manger, will not materially interfere with or detract from fulfillment of the Refuge System Mission or refuge purpose(s).

As stated in the Act, "The mission of the System is to administer a national network of lands and waters for the conservation, management, and where appropriate, restoration of the fish, wildlife, and plant resources and their habitats within the United States for the benefit of present and future generations of Americans."

The Act also requires development of a comprehensive conservation plan for each refuge and management of each refuge consistent with the plan. When writing CCP, planning for expanded or new refuges, and when making management decisions, the Act requires effective coordination with other Federal agencies, state fish and wildlife or conservation agencies, and refuge neighbors. A refuge must also provide opportunities for public involvement when making a compatibility determination or developing a CCP.

National Wildlife Refuge System Volunteer and Community Partnership Enhancement Act of 1998

The Volunteer and Community Partnership Enhancement Act (Public Law 105-242 - Oct. 5, 1998) is intended to enhance volunteer programs, community partnerships and educational programs throughout the National Wildlife Refuge System. The Act proposes the use of several tools to accomplish this task, including pilot projects, cooperative agreements, authorization of funds to carry out programs, written guidance, and status reports. The Act also authorizes the establishment of a Senior Volunteer Corps, consisting of volunteers over 50-years-old.

North American Wetlands Conservation Act (103 Stat. 1968; 16 U.S.C. 4401-4412)

Public Law 101-233, enacted December 13, 1989, provides funding and administrative direction for implementation of the North American Waterfowl Management Plan and the Tripartite Agreement on wetlands between Canada, U.S. and Mexico.

The Act converts the Pittman-Robertson account into a trust fund, with the interest available without appropriation through the year 2006 to carry out the programs authorized by the Act, along with an authorization for annual appropriation of $15 million plus an amount equal to the fines and forfeitures collected under the Migratory Bird Treaty Act.

Available funds may be expended, upon approval of the Migratory Bird Conservation Commission, for payment of not to exceed 50 percent of the United States share of the cost of wetlands conservation projects in Canada, Mexico, or the United States (or 100 percent of the cost of projects on Federal lands). At least 50 percent and no more than 70 percent of the funds received are to go to Canada and Mexico each year.

A North American Wetlands Conservation Council is created to recommend projects to be funded under the Act to the Migratory Bird Conservation Commission. The Council is to be composed of the Director of the Service, the Secretary of the National Fish and Wildlife Foundation, a State fish and game agency director from each Flyway, and three representatives of different non-profit organizations participating in projects under the Plan or the Act. The Chairman of the Council and one other member serve ex officio on the Commission for consideration of the Council's recommendations.

The Commission must justify in writing to the Council and, annually, to Congress, any decisions not to accept Council recommendations.

Oil Pollution Act of 1990

Public Law 101-380 (33 U.S.C. 2701 et seq.; 104 Stat. 484) established new requirements and extensively amended the Federal Water Pollution Control Act (33 U.S.C. 1301 et. seq.) to provide enhanced capabilities for oil spill response and natural resource damage assessment by the Service. It required Service consultation on developing a fish and wildlife response plan for the National Contingency Plan, input to Area Contingency Plans, review of Facility and Tank Vessel Contingency Plans, and to conduct damage assessments associated with oil spills. The following are the pertinent provisions.

Title I, section 1006, provided that Federal trustees shall assess natural resource damages for natural resources under their trusteeship. Federal trustees may, upon request from a State or Indian tribe, assess damages to natural resources for them as well. Trustees shall develop and implement a plan for the restoration, rehabilitation, replacement, or acquisition of the equivalent of natural resources under their trusteeship.

Title I, section 1011, provides that trustees are to be consulted on the appropriate removal action to be taken in connection with any discharge of oil.

Title I, section 1012, provided for the uses of the oil pollution fund. In addition to response costs, the fund may be used without appropriations to pay the costs of assessments, as well as to pay claims for natural resource damages if there are no funds or insufficient funds from a responsible party. (A claims procedure was to be developed under section 1013.) This section also stipulated deadlines for the submission of removal cost claims and damage claims.

Title IV, section 4202, amended subsection 311(j) of the Federal Water Pollution Control Act with respect to the National Planning and Response System. It defined area committees and area contingency plans, and requirements and deadlines for agencies. Under this section, the Service is required to generate a list of all equipment, including fire fighting equipment, as well as personnel and any other equipment and supplies that could be used to expedite the removal of oil or mitigation of a spill.

One aspect of particular interest to the Service involves the identification of ecologically sensitive areas and the preparation of scientific monitoring and evaluation plans. Research conducted by the Service is to be directed and coordinated by the National Wetland Research Center.

Refuge Recreation Act of 1962

This Act authorizes the Secretary of the Interior to administer refuges, hatcheries, and other conservation areas for recreational use, when such uses do not interfere with the area's primary purposes. It authorizes construction and maintenance of recreational facilities and the acquisition of land for incidental fish and wildlife oriented recreational development or protection of natural resources. It also authorizes the charging of fees for public uses.

Refuge Revenue Sharing Act (16 U.S.C. 715s)

Section 401 of the Act of June 15, 1935, (49 Stat. 383) provided for payments to counties in lieu of taxes, using revenues derived from the sale of products from refuges.

Public Law 93-509, approved December 3, 1974, (88 Stat. 1603) required that moneys remaining in the fund after payments be transferred to the Migratory Bird Conservation Fund for land acquisition under provisions of the Migratory Bird Conservation Act.

Public Law 95-469, approved October 17, 1978, (92 Stat. 1319) expanded the revenue sharing system to include National Fish Hatcheries and Service research stations. It also included in the Refuge Revenue Sharing Fund receipts from the sale of salmonid carcasses. Payments to counties were established as:
> 1) on acquired land, the greatest amount calculated on the basis of 75 cents per acre, three-fourths of one percent of the appraised value, or 25 percent of the net receipts produced from the land; and

> 2) on land withdrawn from the public domain, 25 percent of net receipts and basic payments under Public Law 94-565 (31 U.S.C. 1601-1607, 90 Stat. 2662), payment in lieu of taxes on public lands.

This amendment also authorized appropriations to make up any difference between the amount in the Fund and the amount scheduled for payment in any year. The stipulation that payments be used for schools and roads was removed, but counties were required to pass payments along to other units of local government within the county which suffer losses in revenues due to the establishment of Refuges.

Transfer of Certain Real Property for Wildlife Conservation purposes Act of 1948

This Act provides that upon determination by the Administrator of the General Services Administration, real property no longer needed by a Federal agency can be transferred, without reimbursement, to the Secretary of the Interior if the land has particular value for migratory birds, or to a State agency for other wildlife conservation purposes.

Rehabilitation Act of 1973 (29 U.S.C. 794) as amended

Title 5 of P.L. 93-112 (87 Stat. 355), signed October 1, 1973, prohibits discrimination on the basis of handicap under any program or activity receiving Federal financial assistance.

Youth Conservation Corps Act (16 U.S.C. 1701-1706, 84 Stat. 794)

Public Law 91-378, approved August 13, 1970, declares the YCC pilot program a success and establishes permanent programs within the Departments of Interior and Agriculture for young adults who have attained the age of 15, but not the age of 19, to perform specific tasks on lands and waters administered under jurisdiction of these Secretaries. Within the Fish and Wildlife Service, YCC participants perform various tasks on National Wildlife Refuges, National Fish Hatcheries, research stations, and other facilities.

The legislation also authorizes the Secretary of Interior and the Secretary of Agriculture to establish a joint grant program to assist States employing young adults on non-Federal public lands and waters throughout the U.S.

Requires the Secretaries of Interior and Agriculture to prepare a joint report to the President and Congress prior to April 1 of each year.

Wilderness Act of 1964

Public Law 88-577, approved September 3, 1964, directed the Secretary of the Interior, within 10 years, to review every roadless area of 5,000 or more acres and every roadless island (regardless of size) within National Wildlife Refuge and National Park Systems for inclusion in the National Wilderness Preservation System.

Under the Act, federal lands that are declared as Wilderness Areas must be maintained in a natural, undeveloped state in order to "preserve for the American people of present and future generations the benefits of an enduring resource of wilderness." The Act instructs federal agencies to manage Wilderness Areas in a manner which "preserves the wilderness character of the area," and provides "outstanding opportunities for solitude, primitive and unconfined recreation."

Appendix C

Appendix C:

Refuge Cover Type Maps

Eastern Shore of Virginia National Wildlife Refuge
Northampton County, Virginia

N

KEY TO COVERTYPES

Agricultural Field
Beach - Intertidal / Sand
Beach Grass
Beach Grass - Sand
Beach Grass / Iva
Black Locust
Building
Bunker
Cemetery
Cherry
Cherry - Black Locust
Cherry - Pine
Cherry - Sassafras
Cherry / Sassafras
Dune
Emergent Wetland
Firing Range
High Marsh
Iva
Iva or Open Water
Management Field
Mixed Forest

Mixed Oak / Pine
Mixed Pine / Oak
Myrtle
Myrtle - Phragmites
Myrtle / cherry
Open Water
Phragmites
Pine
Pine / Cherry
Road - Parking Area
Rock
Saltmarsh
Sassafras
Sassafras / Pine
Scrub-Shrub
Scrub-Shrub Wetland
Sewage Treatment
Short Grass
Shrub (Privet)
Tideflat
Virginia Pine
Wildlife Plantings

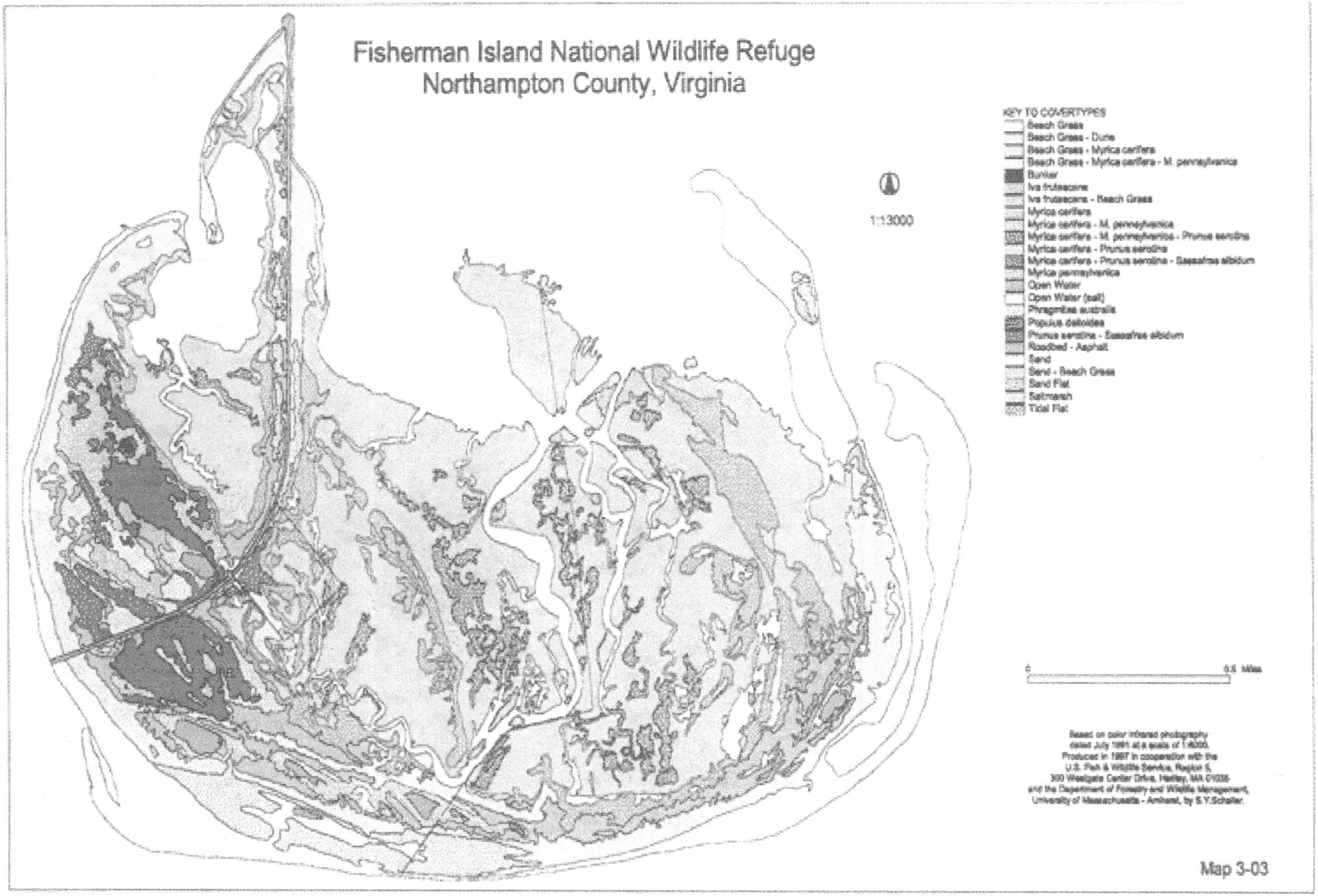

Fisherman Island National Wildlife Refuge
Northampton County, Virginia

Based on color infrared photography
dated July 1997 at a scale of 1:600
Produced in 1997 in cooperation with the
U.S. Fish & Wildlife Service, Region 5
300 Westgate Center Drive, Hadley, MA 01035
and the Department of Forestry and Wildlife Management,
University of Massachusetts - Amherst, by V. Schallner

KEY TO COVERTYPES

Beach Grass
Beach Grass - Dune
Beach Grass - Myrica cerifera
Beach Grass - Myrica cerifera - M. pennsylvanica
Bunker
Iva frutescens - Beach Grass
Iva frutescens
Myrica cerifera
Myrica cerifera - M. pennsylvanica
Myrica cerifera - M. pennsylvanica - Prunus serotina
Myrica cerifera - Prunus serotina
Myrica cerifera - Prunus serotina - Sassafras albidum
Myrica pennsylvanica
Open Water (tidal)
Phragmites australis
Pinus taeda
Prunus serotina - Sassafras albidum
Roadbed - Asphalt
Sand
Sand - Beach Grass
Sand Flat
Saltmarsh
Tidal Flat

1:13000

0.4 Miles

Map 3-03

Appendix D:

Refuge Species List

Birds of the Eastern Shore of Virginia and Fisherman Island Refuges

Season:
s - Spring   March - May
S - Summer   June - August
F - Fall   September - November
W - Winter   December - February

Relative Abundance
a - abundant   a species which is very numerous
c - common   likely to be seen or heard in suitable habitat
u - uncommon   present, but not certain to be seen
o - occasional   seen only a few times during a season
r- rare   may be present but not every year

Common name	Scientific name	s	S	F	W
LOONS - GREBES					
Red-throated Loon	*Gavia stellata*	u		u	u
Common Loon	*Gavia immer*	c	o	c	c
Pied-billed Grebe	*Podilymbus podiceps*	c	o	c	c
Horned Grebe	*Podiceps auritus*	u	o	u	u
Red-necked Grebe	*Podiceps grisegena*	r		r	o
STORM-PETREL					
Wilson's Storm-Petrel	*Oceanites oceanicus*	r	r		
GANNET - PELICANS					
Northern Gannet	*Morus bassanus*	c		o	u
American White Pelican	*Pelecanus erythrorhynchos*	r	r	r	r
•Brown Pelican	Pelecanus occidentalis	c	c	c	r
Great Cormorant	*Phalacrocorax carbo*	u		o	u
Double-crested Cormorant	*Phalacrocorax auritus*	c	c	c	c
BITTERNS -HERONS - IBISES					
American Bittern	Botaurus lentiginosus	u	u	u	u
Least Bittern	*Ixobrychus exilis*		o		
•Great Blue Heron	*Ardea herodias*	c	u	c	u
•Great Egret	*Casmerodius albus*	c	c	c	c
•Snowy Egret	*Egretta thula*	c	c	c	c
•Little Blue Heron	*Egretta caerulea*	c	u	u	o
•Tricolored Heron	*Egretta tricolor*	c	c	c	u
•Cattle Egret	*Bubulcus ibis*	c	c	c	
•Green Heron	*Butorides striatus*	u	c	c	r
•Black-crowned Night-Heron	*Nycticorax nycticorax*	c	c	c	u
•Yellow-crowned Night-Heron	*Nyctanassa violacea* u	u	u	r	
•White Ibis	*Eudocimus albus*	u	o	o	r
•Glossy Ibis	*Plegadis falcinellus*	c	u	u	r
Common name	**Scientific name**	**Seasonal Occurrences**			

		s	*S*	*F*	*W*
Sandhill Crane	*Grus canadensis*	*r*			
SWANS - GEESE - DUCKS					
Tundra Swan	*Cygnus columbianus*	*u*		*u*	*u*
Mute Swan	*Cygnus olor*	*r*			*r*
Snow Goose	*Chen caerulescans*	*u*		*u*	*u*
Brant	*Branta bernicla*	*u*		*u*	*c*
•Canada Goose	*Branta canadensis*	*c*	*u*	*u*	*c*
•Wood Duck	*Aix sponsa*	*u*	*o*	*o*	
Green-winged Teal	*Anas crecca*	*c*	*r*	*u*	*u*
•American Black Duck	*Anas rubripes*	*c*	*u*	*c*	*c*
•Mallard	*Anas platyrhynchos*	*c*	*u*	*c*	*c*
Northern Pintail	*Anas acuta*	*u*		*u*	*u*
Blue-winged Teal	*Anas discors*	*c*	*o*	*c*	*o*
Northern Shoveler	*Anas clypeata*	*c*		*u*	*u*
•Gadwall	*Anas strepera*	*c*	*u*	*u*	*u*
Eurasian Wigeon	*Anas penelope*				*r*
American Wigeon	*Anas americana*	*u*		*u*	*u*
Canvasback	*Aythya valisineria*	*o*		*o*	*o*
Redhead	*Aythya americana*	*o*		*o*	*o*
Ring-necked Duck	*Aythya collaris*	*o*		*o*	*u*
Greater Scaup	*Aythya marila*	*u*		*u*	*u*
Lesser Scaup	*Aythya affinis*	*u*		*u*	*u*
Common Eider	*Somateria mollissima*				*r*
King Eider	*Somateria spectabilis*				*r*
Harlequin Duck	*Histrionicus histrionicus*	*r*			*r*
Oldsquaw	*Clangula hyemalis*	*u*		*u*	*u*
Black Scoter	*Melanitta nigra*	*u*		*u*	*c*
Surf Scoter	*Melanitta perspicillata*	*c*	*r*	*c*	*c*
White-winged Scoter	*Melanitta fusca*	*u*		*u*	*u*
Common Goldenye	*Bucephala clangula*				*u*
Bufflehead	*Bucephala albeola*	*c*		*c*	*c*
Hooded Merganser	*Lophodytes cucullatus*	*c*		*u*	*u*
Common Merganser	*Mergus merganser*				*u*
Red-breasted Merganser	*Mergus serrator*	*c*	*r*	*c*	*c*
Ruddy Duck	*Oxyura jamaicensis*	*o*		*u*	*u*
VULTURES - HAWKS - FALCONS					
Black Vulture	*Coragypus atratus* *c*	*u*	*c*	*u*	
Turkey Vulture	*Cathartes aura*	*c*	*u*	*c*	*c*
•Osprey	*Pandion haliaetus*	*c*	*c*	*c*	*r*
Mississippi Kite	*Ictinia mississippiensis*	*r*	*r*		

Common name	**Scientific name**	**Seasonal Occurrences**

Common name	Scientific name	s	S	F	W
Bald Eagle	*Haliaeetus leucocephalus*	u	u	u	u
Golden Eagle	*Aquila chrysaetos*			r	r
•Northern Harrier	*Circus cyaneus*	c	o	c	c
Sharp-shinned Hawk	*Accipiter striatus*	u		a	u
Cooper's Hawk	*Accipiter cooperii*	u		u	u
Northern Goshawk	*Accipiter gentilis*			r	r
Red-shouldered Hawk	*Buteo lineatus*	u	o	u	u
Broad-winged Hawk	*Buteo platypterus*	u		c	
Swainson's Hawk	*Buteo swainsoni*			r	
•Red-tailed Hawk	*Buteo jamaicensis*	c	u	c	c
Rough-legged Hawk	*Buteo lagopus*	r		r	r
American Kestrel	*Falco sparverius*	u	u	a	u
Merlin	*Falco columbarius*	u		c	u
•Peregrine Falcon	*Falco peregrinus*	u	u	c	u
QUAIL					
Ring-necked Pheasant	*Phasianus colchicus*	o	o	o	o
•Northern Bobwhite	*Colinus virginianus*	c	c	c	c
Wild Turkey	*Meleagris gallopavo*	u	u	u	u
RAILS - CRANES					
Yellow Rail	*Coturnicops noveboracensis*			r	
Black Rail	*Laterallus jamaicensis*			r	
•Clapper Rail	*Rallus longirostris*	c	c	a	u
King Rail	*Rallus elegans*	u	o	u	u
Virginia Rail	*Rallus limicola*	u	u	u	u
Sora	*Porzana carolina*	u		u	o
Common Moorhen	*Gallinula chloropus*	o	o	o	r
American Coot	*Fulica americana*	u		u	u
PLOVERS SANDPIPERS					
Black-bellied Plover	*Pluvialis squatarola*	c	o	c	u
Lesser Golden Plover	*Pluvialis dominica*		o	o	
Semipalmated Plover	*Charadrius semipalmatus*	c	o	c	o
•Piping Plover	*Charadrius melodus*	u	u	u	r
•Killdeer	*Charadrius vociferus*	c	u	u	u
•American Oystercatcher	*Haematopus palliatus*	c	c	c	c
American Avocet	*Recurvirostra americana*	r		r	r
Black-necked Stilt	*Himantopus mexicanus*	o	r		
Greater Yellowlegs	*Tringa melanoleuca*	c	o	c	u
Lesser Yellowlegs	*Tringa flavipes*	u	o	c	u
Solitary Sandpiper	*Tringa solitaria*	u	u	u	
•Willet	*Catoptrophorus semipalmatus*	c	c	c	u

Common name	Scientific name	Seasonal Occurrences

		s	S	F	W
Spotted Sandpiper	*Actitis macularia*	c	u	c	r
Upland Sandpiper	*Bartramia longicauda*	o	u	u	
Whimbrel	*Numenius phaeopus*	u	u	u	o
Marbled Godwit	*Limosa fedoa*		o	o	o
Ruddy Turnstone	*Arenaria interpres*	u	u	u	u
Red Knot	*Calidris canutus*	u	u	u	r
Sanderling	*Caladris alba*	c	u	c	c
Semipalmated Sandpiper	*Calidris pusilla*	c	u	u	
Western Sandpiper	*Calidris mauri*	u	u	u	u
Least Sandpiper	*Calidris minutilla*	c	u	u	r
White-rumped Sandpiper	*Calidris fuscicollis*	u	u	u	
Pectoral Sandpiper	*Calidris acuminata*	u	u	u	
Dunlin	*Calidrus tenuirostris*	c	o	c	c
Stilt Sandpiper	*Calidrus himantopus*	o	u	u	
Buff-breasted Sandpiper	*Tryngites subruficollis*		o	o	
Short-billed Dowitcher	*Limnodromus griseus*	c	u	c	o
Long-billed Dowitcher	*Limnodromus scolopaceus*		o	o	o
Common Snipe	*Gallinago gallinago*	c		u	u
•American Woodcock	*Scolopax minor*	u	o	c	a
Wilson's Phalarope	*Phalaropus tricolor*		o	o	

GULLS - TERNS

		s	S	F	W
•Laughing Gull	*Larus atricilla*	a	a	a	o
Bonaparte's Gull	*Larus phildelphia*	u		u	u
Ring-billed Gull	*Larus delawarensis*	c	o	c	c
•Herring Gull	*Larus argentatus*	a	c	a	a
Lesser Black-backed Gull	*Larus fuscus*	r		o	o
•Greater Black-backed Gull	*Larus marinus*	c	u	u	c
Iceland Gull	*Larus glaucoides*	r			
Gull-billed Tern	*Sterna nilotica*	u	u	u	
•Caspian Tern	*Sterna caspia*	u	u	c	
•Royal Tern	*Sterna maxima*	a	a	c	r
•Sandwich Tern	*Sterna sandvicensis*	o	o	o	
•Common Tern	*Sterna hirundo*	u	u	c	
•Forster's Tern	*Sterna forsteri*	c	u	a	o
Least Tern	*Sterna antillarum*	u	u	o	
Black tern	*Chlidonias niger*	o	o	u	
Black Skimmer	*Rynchops niger*	c	c	c	r

DOVES - CUCKOOS - OWLS - SWIFTS - HUMMINGBIRDS

		s	S	F	W
•Rock Dove	*Columba livia*	u	c	c	c
•Mourning Dove	*Zenaida macroura*	c	c	c	c
Black-billed Cuckoo	*Coccyzus erythropthalmus*			o	
•Yellow-billed Cuckoo	*Coccyzus americanus*	o		u	u
•Barn Owl	*Tyto alba*	u	u	u	u
•Eastern Screech-Owl	*Otus asio*	u	c	c	c

Common name	Scientific name	s	S	F	W
•Great Horned Owl	*Bubo virginianus*	c	c	c	c
Long-eared Owl	*Asio otus*			o	o
Short-eared Owl	*Asio flammeus*	o		u	u
Northern Saw-whet Owl	*Aegolius acadicus*			o	c
Common Nighthawk	*Chordeiles minor*	u	u	u	
•Chuck-will's widow	*Caprimulgus carolinensis*	u	c	o	
Whip-poor-will	*Caprimulgus vociferus*	o		o	
Chimney Swift	*Chaetura pelagica*	u	u	c	
•Ruby-throated Hummingbird	*Archilochus colubris*	c	u	u	
Belted Kingfisher	*Ceryle alcyon*	c	o	c	u

WOODPECKERS - FLYCATCHERS

Common name	Scientific name	s	S	F	W
Red-headed Woodpecker	*Melanerpes erythrocepthalus*	o	o	u	o
•Red-bellied Woodpecker	*Melanerpes carolinus*	c	u	u	u
Yellow-bellied Sapsucker	*Sphyrapicus ruber*	o		u	u
•Downy Woodpecker	*Picoides pubenscens*	c	c	c	o
•Hairy Woodpecker	*Picoides villosus*	u	u	u	u
•Northern Flicker	*Colaptes auratus*	c	c	a	c
Pileated Woodpecker	*Dryocopus pileatus*	u	o	o	o
Olive-sided Flycatcher	*Contopus borealis*	r		r	
•Eastern Wood-Pewee	*Contopus virens*	u	u	u	
Yellow-bellied Flycatcher	*Empidonax flaviventris*			u	
Acadian Flycatcher	*Empidonax virescens*	o	o	u	
Alder Flycatcher	*Empidonax alnorum*			u	
Willow Flycatcher	*Empidonax traillii*			u	
Least Flycatcher	*Empidonax minimus*	o		u	
•Eastern Phoebe	*Sayornis phoebe*	c	o	c	o
Say's Phoebe	*Sayornis saya*				r
•Great Crested Flycatcher	*Myiarchus crinitus*	c	u	u	
Western Kingbird	*Tyrannus verticalis*			o	r
Eastern Kingbird	*Tyrannus tyrannus*	c	c	a	
Scissor-tailed Flycatcher	*Tyrannus forficatus*		r	r	

LARKS - SWALLOWS - JAYS - CROWS

Common name	Scientific name	s	S	F	W
Horned Lark	*Eremophila alpestris*	u		u	u
•Purple Martin	*Progne subis*	c	c	u	
•Tree Swallow	*Tachycineta bicolor*	c	c	a	o
Northern Rough-winged Swallow	*Stelgidopteryx serripennis*	u	u	u	
Bank Swallow	*Riparia riparia*	u	u	c	
Cliff Swallow	*Hirundo pyrrhonota*	o	o	u	
•Barn Swallow	*Hirundo rustica*	c	a	a	
•Blue Jay	*Cyanocitta cristata*	u	u	a	c
•American Crow	*Corvus brachyrhynchos*	c	o	c	c
•Fish Crow	*Corvus ossifragus*	c	c	a	c

TITMICE - NUTHATCHES - WRENS

Common name	Scientific name	s	S	F	W
•Carolina Chickadee	*Parus carolinensis*	c	c	c	c

Common name	Scientific name	Seasonal Occurrences			
		s	S	F	W

Common name	Scientific name	s	S	F	W
•Tufted Titmouse	*Parus bicolor*	u	u	u	u
Red-breasted Nuthatch	*Sitta canadensis*	u		c	c
White-breasted Nuthatch	*Sitta carolinensis*	o		u	u
•Brown-headed Nuthatch	*Sitta pusilla*	u	o	u	u
Brown Creeper	*Certhia americana*	u		c	u
•Carolina Wren	*Thryothorus ludovicianus*	c	c	c	c
•House Wren	*Troglodytes aedon*	u	u	c	u
Winter Wren	*Troglodytes troglodytes*	u		u	u
Sedge Wren	*Cistothorus platensis*	u		u	u
Marsh Wren	*Cistothorus palustris*	u	u	c	u

KINGLETS - THRUSHES - THRASHERS

Common name	Scientific name	s	S	F	W
Golden-crowned Kinglet	*Regulus satrapa*	u		c	c
Ruby-crowned Kinglet	*Regulus calendula*	u		a	c
•Blue-gray Gnatcatcher	*Polioptila caerulea*	c	o	u	r
•Eastern Bluebird	*Sialia sialis*	c	u	c	u
Veery	*Catharus fuscescens*	u		c	
Gray-cheeked Thrush	*Catharus minimus*	u		u	
Swainson's Thrush	*Catharus ustulatus*	u		c	
Binknell's Thrush	*Catharus minimus*	o			
Hermit Thrush	*Catharus guttatus*	u		c	u
Wood Thrush	*Hylocichla mustelina*	u	o	u	
•American Robin	*Turdus migratorius*	c	c	a	c
•Gray Catbird	*Dumetella carolinensis*	c	c	c	u
•Northern Mockingbird	*Mimus polyglottos*	c	c	c	u
•Brown Thrasher	*Toxostoma rufum*	u	u	c	u

WAXWINGS - SHRIKE - STARLING

Common name	Scientific name	s	S	F	W
American Pipit	*Anthus rubescens*	u		c	u
Cedar Waxwing	*Bombycilla garrulus*	c	o	c	u
Loggerhead Shrike	*Lanius ludovicianus*	r		r	r
•European Starling	*Sternus vulgaris*	a	a	a	a

VIREO - WOOD WARBLERS

Common name	Scientific name	s	S	F	W
•White-eyed Vireo	*Vireo atricapillus*	c	u	c	r
Blue-headed Vireo	*Vireo solitarius*	u		u	r
Yellow-throated Vireo	*Vireo flavifrons*	o		r	
Warbling Vireo	*Vireo gilvus*	o		r	
Philadelphia Vireo	*Vireo philadelphicus*	o		r	
•Red-eyed Vireo	*Vireo olivaceus*	u	u	c	
Blue-winged Warbler	*Vermivora pinus*	o		u	
Golden-winged Warbler	*Vermivora chrysoptera*			r	
Tenessee Warbler	*Vermivora peregrina*	o		u	
Orange-crowned Warbler	*Vermivora celata*	o		o	u
Nashville Warbler	*Vermivora ruficapilla*		o		u

Common name	Scientific name	Seasonal Occurrences			
		s	S	F	W
Northern Parula	*Parula americana*	c		u	

Common name	Scientific name	s	S	F	W
Yellow Warbler	*Dendroica petechia*	c	u	c	
Chestnut-sided Warbler	*Dendroica pensylvanica*	u		u	
Magnolia Warbler	*Dendroica magnolia*	u		c	
Cape May Warbler	*Dendroica tigrina*	o		c	
Black-throated Blue Warbler	*Dendroica caerulescens*	c		c	
Yellow-rumped Warbler	*Dendroica coronata*	a		a	a
Black-throated Green Warbler	*Dendroica virens*	u		u	
Blackburian Warbler	*Dendroica fusca*	o		u	
Yellow-throated Warbler	*Dendroica dominica*	u		o	
•Pine Warbler	*Dendroica pinus*	c	c	c	u
•Prarie Warbler	*Dendroica discolor*	c	u	c	r
Palm Warbler	*Dendroica palmarum u*		c	u	
Bay-breasted warbler	*Dendroica castanae*	o		u	
Blackpoll Warbler	*Dendroica striata*	u		c	
Cerulean Warbler	*Dendroica cerulea*		r		
Black-and-White Warbler	*Mniotilta varia*	u		c	r
American Redstart	*Setophaga ruticilla*	c		a	
Prothonotary Warbler	*Protonotaria citrea*	o		o	
Worm-eating Warbler	*Helmitheros vernivorus*	o		u	
Ovenbird	*Seiurus aurocapillus*	c	o	a	r
Northern Waterthrush	*Seiurus noveboracensis*	u	u	c	
Louisiana Waterthrush	*Seiurus motacilla*	o	r	r	
Kentucky Warbler	*Oporornis formosus*	o		o	
Connecticut Warbler	*Oporornis agilis*			u	
Mourning Warbler	*Oporornis philadelphia*	o		u	
•Common Yellowthroat	*Geothlypis trichas*	c	c	a	o
Hooded Warbler	*Wilsonia citrina*	o		o	
Wilson' Warbler	*Wilsonia pusilla*	u		u	
Canada warbler	*Wilsonia canadensis*	u		u	
•Yellow-breasted Chat	*Icteria virens*	c	u	u	o

TANAGERS - SPARROWS

Common name	Scientific name	s	S	F	W
•Summer Tanager	*Piranga rubra*	u	u	u	
Scarlet Tanager	*Piranga olivacea*	u		u	
•Northern Cardinal	*Cardinalis cardinalis*	c	c	c	c
Rose-breasted Grosbeak	*Pheucticus ludovicianus*	o		u	
•Blue Grosbeak	*Guiraca caerulea*	c	u	u	
•Indigo Bunting	*Passerina cyanea*	c	u	c	
Dickcissel	*Spiza americana*	o		c	
•Eastern Towhee	*Pipilo erythrophthalmus*	c	u	a	c
American Tree Sparrow	*Spizella arborea*	r			r
Clay-colored Sparrow	*Spizella pallida*			r	
•Chipping Sparrow	*Spizella passerina*	u	o	c	o

Common name	**Scientific name**	**Seasonal Occurrences**			
		s	*S*	*F*	*W*
•Field Sparrow	*Spizella pusilla*	c	u	c	u
Vesper Sparrow	*Pooecetes gramineus*	o		u	u

Lark Sparrow	*Chondestes grammacus*			r	
Savanna Sparrow	*Passerculus sandwichensis*	u		c	c
•Grasshopper Sparrow	*Ammodramus savannarum*	u	o	u	
Heslow's Sparrow	*Ammodramus henslowii*		r		
Saltmarsh Sharp-tailed Sparrow	*Ammodramus caudacutusc*		o	u	u
•Seaside Sparrow	*Ammodramus maritimus*	c	u	a	u
Fox Sparrow	*Passerella iliaca*	o		u	u
•Song Sparrow	*Melospiza melodia*	c	u	c	a
Lincoln's Sparrow	*Melospiza lincolnii*	r		r	r
Swamp Sparrow	*Melospiza georgiana*	c		a	c
White-throated Sparrow	*Zonotrichia albicollis*	c		a	a
White-crowned Sparrow	*Zonotrichia leucophrys*	o		o	o
Dark-eyed Junco	*Junco hyemalis*	u		u	u
Lapland Longspur	*Calcarius lapponicus*			o	o
Snow Bunting	*Plectrophenax nivalis*			o	o

BLACKBIRDS - FINCHES

Bobolink	*Dolichonyx oryzivorus*	u	o	a	
•Red-winged Blackbird	*Agelaius phoeniceus*	c	c	a	c
•Eastern Meadowlark	*Sturnell magna*	c	u	c	c
Rusty Blackbird	*Euphagus carolinus*	o		c	u
Brewer's Blackbird	*Euphagus cyanocephalus*				r
•Boat-tailed Grackle	*Quiscalus major*	c	c	a	c
•Common Grackle	*Quiscalus quiscula*	a	a	c	c
•Brown-headed Cowbird	*Molothrus ater*	c	u	c	u
•Orchard Oriole	*Icterus spurius*	c	u	r	
Baltimore Oriole	*Icterus galbula*	u		c	r
Purple Finch	*Carpodacus purpureus*	o		u	u
•House Finch	*Carpodacus mexicanus*	c	o	u	u
Red Crossbill	*Loxia curvirostra*			o	o
White-winged Crossbill	*Loxia leucoptera*				r
Common Redpoll	*Carduelis flammea*				r
Pine Siskin	*Carduelis pinus*	o		c	c
•American Goldfinch	*Carduelis tristis*	c	c	a	c
Evening Grosbeak	*Coccothraustes vespertinus*			u	u
•House Sparrow	*Passer domesticus*	u	u	u	u

Reptiles and Amphibians of the Eastern Shore of Virginia Refuge

Frogs and Toads
Eastern Cricket Frog	*Acris crepitans*
Eastern American toad	*Bufo americanus*
Fowler's toad	*Bufo fowleri*
Cope's gray treefrog	*Hyla chrysoscelis*
Northern spring peeper	*Pseudacris crucifer*
New Jersey chorus frog	*Pseudacris feriarum kalmi*
Southern green frog	*Rana clamitans melonata*
Southern leopard frog	*Rana sphenocephala utricularius*
American bullfrog	*Rana catesbeiana*
Pickerel frog	*Rana palustris*
Eastern narrow-mouthed toad	*Gastrophryne carolinensis*

Freshwater, Sea, and Estuarine turtles
Eastern painted turtle	*Chrysemys picta*
Spotted turtle	*Clemmys guttata*
Eastern mud turtle	*Kinsternon subrubrum*
Northern red-bellied cooter	*Pseudemys rubriventris*
Eastern box turtle	*Terrapene carolina*
Eastern snapping turtle	*Chelydra serpintina*
Loggerhead sea turtle	*Caretta caretta*
Green sea turtle	*Chelonia mydas*
Leatherback sea turtle	*Dermochelys coriacea*
Kemp's Ridley sea turtle	*Lepidochelys kempii*
Northern diamond-backed terrpin	*Malaclemys terrapin*

Salamanders
Red-backed salamander	*Plethodon cinercus*
Red-spotted Newt	*Notophthalmus viridescens*

Lizards
Little brown skink	*Scincella lateralis*
Broad-headed skink	*Eumeces laticeps*
Northern fence lizard	*Sceloporus undulatus hyacinthinus*
Five-lined skink	*Eumeces fasciatus*

Snakes
Northern black racer	*Coluber constrictor*
Black rat snake	*Elaphe obsoleta*
Eastern hognose snake	*Heterodon platirhinos*
Common kingsnake	*Lampropeltis getula*
Northern watersnake	*Nerodia sipedon*
Rough greensnake	*Opheodrys aestivus*
Northern brownsnake	*Storeria dekayi*
Eastern ribbonsnake	*Thamnophis sauritus*

Eastern gartersnake	*Thamnophis sirtalis*
Northern copperhead	*Agkistrodon contortrix mokasen*
Eastern wormsnake	*Carphophis amoenus*

Mammals of the Eastern Shore of Virginia and Fisherman Island Refuges

white-tailed deer	*Odocoileus virginianus*
coyote	*Canis latrans*
gray fox	*Urocyon cinereoargenteus*
red fox	*Vulpes vulpes*
raccoon	*Procyon lotor*
river otter	*Lutra canadensis*
American mink	*Mustela vison*
muskrat	*Ondatra zibethicus*
eastern cotton-tail	*Sylvilagus floridanus*
Hutchen's cotton-tail	*Sylvilagus floridanu hutchensi* (likely extirpated)
Virginia opossum	*Didelphis virginiana*
southern flying squirrel	*Glaucomys volans*
gray squirrel	*Sciurus carolinensis*
marsh rice rat	*Oryzomys palustris*
Norway rat	*Rattus norvegicus*
black rat	*Rattus rattus*
meadow vole	*Microtus pennsylvanicus*
pine vole	*Microtus pinetorum*
northern short-tailed shrew	*Blarina brevicauda*
least shrew	*Cryptotis parva*
star-nosed mole	*Condylura cristata*
Eastern mole	*Scalopus aquaticus*
white-footed mouse	*Peromyscus leucopus*
meadow jumping mouse	*Zapus hudsonicus*
house mouse	*Mus musculus*
big brown bat	*Eptesicus fuscus*
silver-haired bat	*Lasionycteris noctivagans*
Eastern red bat	*Lasuirus borealis*
hoary bat	*Lasiurus cinereus*
little brown myotis	*Myotis lucifugus*
Northern myotis	*Myotis septentrionalis*
Eastern pipistrella	*Pipistrella subflavus*
evening bat	*Nycticeius humeralis*

Marine mammals

Harbor Seal	*Phoca vitulina*
Fin-backed Whale	*Balaenoptera physalus*
Sei Whale	*Balaenoptera borealis*
Hump-backed Whale	*Megaptera novaeangliae*
Atlantic Right Whale	*Balaena glacialis*

Butterflies and Skippers of the Eastern Shore of Virginia and Fisherman Island Refuges

Giant Swallowtail	*Papilio cresphontes*
Eastern Tiger Swallowtail	*Papilio glaucus*
Spicebush Swallowtail	*Papilio troilus*
Black Swallowtail	*Papilio polyxenes*
Palamedes Swallowtail	*Papilio palamedes*
Pipevine Swallowtail	*Battus philenor*
Cabbage White	*Pieris rapae*
Falcate Orange-tip	*Anthocharis midea*
Clouded (Common) Sulphur	*Colias philodice*
Orange Sulphur	*Colias eurytheme*
Cloudless Giant Sulphur	*Phoebis sennae*
Little Yellow	*Eurema lisa*
Sleepy Orange	*Eurema nicippe*
American Copper	*Lycaena phlaeas*
Red-banded Hairstreak	*Calycopis cecrops*
Gray Hairstreak	*Strymon melinus*
Eastern Tailed Blue	*Everes comyntas*
Spring Azure	*Celastrina ariolus*
Brown Elfin	*Incisalia augustinus*
Frosted Elfin	*Incisalia irus*
Henry's Elfin	*Incisalia henrici*
Eastern Pine Elfin	*Incisalia niphon*
Snout Butterfly	*Libytheana carinenta*
Gulf Fritillary	*Agraulis vanillae*
Variegated Fritillary	*Euptoieta claudia*
Pearl Crescent	*Phciodes tharos*
Question Mark	*Polygonia interrogationis*
Comma	*Polygonia comma*
Mourning Cloak	*Nymphalis antiopa*
American Lady	*Vanessa virginiensis*
Painted Lady	*Vanessa cardui*
Red Admiral	*Vanessa atalanta*
Buckeye	*Junonia coenia*
Red-spotted Purple	*Limentitis arthemis astyanax*
Viceroy	*Limenitis archippus*
Hackberry Butterfly	*Asterocampa celtis*
Tawny Emperor	*Asterocampa clyton*
Little Wood Satyr	*Megisto cymela*
Large Wood Nymph	*Cercyonis pegala*
Monarch	*Danaus plexippus*
Silver-spotted Skipper	*Epargyreus clarus*
Long-tailed Skipper	*Urbanus proteus*
Juvenal's Duskywing	*Erynnis juvenalis*
Horace's Duskywing	*Erynnis horatius*
Wild Indigo Duskywing	*Erynnis baptisiae*

Checkered Skipper	*Pyrgus communis*
Common Sootywing	*Pholisora catullus*
Swarthy Skipper	*Nastra Iherminier*
Clouded Skipper	*Lerema accius*
Least Skipper	*Ancyloxypha numitor*
Fiery Skipper	*Hylephila phyleus*
Tawny-edged Skipper	*Polites themistocles*
Crossline Skipper	*Polites origenes*
Southern Broken Dash	*Wallengrenia otho*
Northern Broken Dash	*Wallengrenia egeremet*
Little Glassywing	*Pompeius verna*
Sachem	*Atalopedes campestris*
Zabulon Skipper	*Poanes zabulon*
Aaron's Skipper	*Poanes aaroni*
Broad-winged Skipper	*Poanes viator*
Dun Skipper	*Euphyes vestris*
Common Roadside Skipper	*Amblyscirtes vialis*
Saltmarsh Skipper	*Panoquina panoquin*
Long-winged (Ocola) Skipper	*Panoquina ocola*

Appendix E

Appendix E:

Cultural Resources

Eastern Shore of Virginia National Wildlife Refuge

Cultural Resource Sites and Structures

Information about the 11 known archaeological sites at Eastern Shore of Virginia National Wildlife Refuge comes from the Service's Region 5 Cultural Resource Inventory. This consists of site forms, results of field work, and map locations. Table E-1 summarizes the known archaeological sites and historic structures showing whether they are eligible for the National Register, their Service and state site inventory numbers, and a brief description.

One Eastern Shore of Virginia Refuge cultural resource site tested in 1988 is likely to be eligible for the National Register. This is a historic site with three standing structures, and substantial intact archaeological deposits. The buildings are in serious disrepair. The site also contains archaeological and historic resources. The house is a reminder of the early history of the eastern shore. While the farmstead has historic significance which may make it eligible for the National Register, the condition of the structures has deteriorated since their identification in 1988 and this may affect its current eligibility.

In addition to the site discussed in Table H-1, there are structures remaining on the refuge from the World War II era coastal defenses of Fort John Custis, which may be eligible for the National Register. According to a 1994 visit report (Adams and Wiles 1994) these structures include the following:

■ Battery 9, Construction number 228, which was once equipped with two 6-inch guns. The two gun pits have been filled for safety reasons. The battery, or bunker, contains no original equipment. The refuge uses the building for storage.

■ Battery 12, Winslow Battery. This battery contained two 16-inch guns. A Battery Control Station is on top of the battery. The two casemates of the battery are open, and a main corridor connects them. The corridor has been fenced off for safety reasons. I beam shell rails remain in the shell rooms and main corridor, and the unusual feature of freshwater tanks and pump next to the engine   room. Dr E. Raymond Lewis, an historian, librarian, and authority on coastal artillery who visited the Fort in 1975 felt that such intact ceiling mounted ammunition tracks are rare.

Known Cultural Resources at Eastern Shore of Virginia and Fisherman Island Refuges				
FWS Number	State Number	Name	National Register Eligibility	Description
ESV-001P	44-NH-231		No	Surface lithics
ESV-002G		Fitchett/Hallett Graveyard	No	Cemetery
ESV-003H		Edna L. Fitchett Farm Site	No	Site of demolished farm buildings now gravel pit
ESV-004G	44-NH280		No	Two grave cemetery
ESV-005H	44-NH-232	Hallett Farm Site	No	Two foundations, one brick and one brick and concrete. No intact subsurface deposits
ESV-006H	44-NH-281	Hillary G. Fitchett Farm Site	No	No structural remains or subsurface features. One sherd
ESV-007H	44-NH-282		No	60 x10 meter artifact concentration. No intact deposits or structural remains
ESV-008H	44-NH-283		No	100 meter sq. area with surface and subsurface turn of 20th century artifacts
ESV-009S	Includes 44-NH-383 and 384	Fort John Custis	Possibly	Four structures on Fisherman's Island and five on Eastern Shore of Virginia NWR
ESV-010S and H	44-NH-285		Possibly	Two houses and an outbuilding. Intact surface and subsurface historic deposits
ESV-011H	44-NH-230	Cape Charles Dump Site	No	Surface 20th century artifacts

Table E-1. Known archaeological sites and historic structures on Eastern Shore of Virginia Refuge, includuing the site's Service and State number, the name of the site, its eligibility for the National Register, and a brief description.

■   Plotting and Switchboard Room for Battery 12, north of the battery. In 1975, the Air Force converted this feature to a noncommissioned Officers Club.

■   One of four earth berms constructed as a backstop for the rifle range, currently used by the refuge as a shooting range.

■   A concrete fire control tower at Battery 8, two 8-inch railway gun emplacements which are now gone. Rails have been removed, and there is no structural evidence other than the tower.

Remains of two other Fort John Custis features which have been removed were located and documented in 1992, as part of the Espey, Huston and Associates study of the parallel crossing. These remains are not eligible for the National Register. They include:

■   footings and slabs of a radar tower near Wise Point.
■   boat ramp and combination switching and cable shed at Wise Point.

Other structures related to Fort John Custis were removed soon after the Service acquired the Air Force Station. The Service owns structures related to this Fort on Fisherman Island as well. These are described in the section about Fisherman Island Refuge (below). None of the structures at Eastern Shore of Virginia Refuge were evaluated for National Register eligibility as part of the Goodwin archaeological study in 1988, or as part of the Navy-sponsored study of 1983. No alterations to the structures are planned, and no further demolition is anticipated.

There is one known prehistoric archaeological site, identified in 1982 (Mayne, no date) based on 17 surface prehistoric artifacts and two clay pipe stems. None of these artifacts are clearly diagnostic of a time period. A 1988 archaeological survey (Goodwin et al. 1989) produced an additional artifact, but nine test pits excavated near this item produced no subsurface remains. The contractor concluded this site was not eligible for listing in the National Register because its thinly scattered, shallow deposits had been disturbed by plowing and the site had no further information potential.

Four historic archaeological sites containing artifacts were also tested in 1988 (Goodwin et al. 1989) and found not eligible for the National Register. A 20th century domestic dump, perhaps redeposited by the Army during clearing activities, is also not likely to produce important information, and therefore is not eligible for the National Register.

Two other sites include an historic cemetery used by the Fitchett and Hallett families, and the site of a house which belonged to Miss Edna Linder Fitchett in 1915. The house was removed when the Army acquired the land in the 1940s. The house site has been disturbed for use as a borrow pit during construction of a nearby battery during World War II. It has no potential to give information about the past, and is not eligible for the National Register. Two intermarried families used the cemetery between 1856 and 1936. The cemetery by itself is not eligible for the National Register, but serves as a tangible reminder of the refuge's past.

A second cemetery with two graves was located nearby in 1940. It has not been located by recent cultural resource surveys, but has been filled and it is likely that it still exists underground, unmarked. It also would not be eligible for the National Register.

Because Eastern Shore of Virginia Refuge has not been completely surveyed, these eleven known cultural resources are likely to be only a subset of all archaeological sites on the refuge. Ground disturbing work on the refuge needs review by the Regional Historic Preservation Officer.

Predicting Site Locations

The Goodwin study (Goodwin et al. 1989) also produced a land form map showing the extent of modern coastal sands, tidal marshes, remnants of Pleistocene (between 10,000 and 1.8 million years ago) terrain, and Sangamon (about 100,000 years ago) land forms on the lower eastern shore (Goodwin et al. 1989:23). The contractor felt modern coastal sands are unlikely to contain intact sites, and did not include them in the survey. Sites in tidal marshes will be difficult to locate because of the water, and therefore, the marshes were excluded. The remaining Sangamon and Pleistocene landforms are considered likely to contain as yet undiscovered archaeological sites.

In addition, Goodwin and Associates conducted a limited field survey of the land forms to test the likelihood of finding sites on Sangamon and Pleistocene landforms. The study concluded that there are likely to be more sites than we currently know of in these two landform categories.

Fisherman Island NWR

Cultural Resource Sites and Structures

Fisherman Island Refuge, as well as Eastern Shore of Virginia Refuge, contains the structural remains of part of Fort John Custis. In 1975, there were 16 structures remaining on Fisherman Island from the Fort (Virant 1975), which operated during World War II. The island may also contain the buried remains of World War I defenses and a late 19th century U.S. Health Department quarantine station. Reportedly, at Fishermans Island's core are the remains of the Willam Knight, a circa 1820 shipwreck which is reported to have initiated the accumulation of the island.

By 1858, the Commonwealth of Virginia was releasing its title to three newly forming islands which are now part of Fisherman Island. By 1884, Fisherman Island was being used as a quarantine station through an arrangement with the State. In 1891, the northwestern most of the three, Linen Bar, was acquired through condemnation by the U. S. Health Department for a quarantine station (U. S. Fish and Wildlife Service Land Acquisition Records). By 1894, there were seven buildings at the station.

By 1911, the War Department was seeking to acquire part of Fishermans Island for gun emplacements to defend Baltimore Harbor and the coast.

In 1912, the U. S. successfully pressed a civil suit for an injunction against Carmen Skidmore and others. The government first pressed an unsuccessful criminal suit. The men had rented the right to clam on William Knight Shoals for three months. They constructed a cabin near the quarantine station boundary and used it as a base to trespass on government land and clam at clamming grounds there. After several warnings, the trespassers were arrested. As part of this court case against Skidmore, the government had a 1906 surveyed boundary of Fisherman Island marked with iron pins. The defendants were enjoined to stop trespassing on the land defined by the pins. Skidmore's home is part of Eastern Shore of Virginia Refuge, and is one of its known cultural resource sites.

In 1917, the Army brought four five-inch guns to Fisherman Island. Barracks were constructed on Fisherman and William Knight Shoals Island, where search lights were located.

In 1940, the Army acquired land at Wise Point for a fort. Within 12 days of Pearl Harbor, on December 19, 1941, the fort was garrisoned with the 246th Coast Artillery Regiment and mobile railway mounted guns were moved to the site. Beginning in 1942, Fort John Custis included gun emplacements on Fisherman, as well as at Wise Point. The Fort and Harbor Defenses of Chesapeake Bay were inactivated in 1950.

The Air Force occupied and altered Fort John Custis from 1950 until 1983. By 1994, only four World War II structures remained visible on the surface of Fisherman Island (Adams 1994). The 1994 visible structures were:

■ Battery 11, construction 227, a 6-inch gun emplacement. Guns once mounted here are at Gulf Islands National Sea Shore, at Fort Pickins. The Battery Commander Station, a tower, blown up by the Navy during Service ownership, is lying nearby. Air compressors, generators, and chemical warfare decontamination equipment remained in the Battery in 1994. Only two other World War II batteries contain their equipment.

■ Battery 20, an emplacement for two 3-inch guns intended for use against submarines and torpedos. The original guns were relocated to Fort Story at Cape Henry in 1944. A search light tower and control tower associated with this battery were also demolished during Service ownership, and may remain at the site. In 1994, the magazine for this battery was being used by the Service. Battery 24 replaced this battery.

■ Battery 24, built in 1943, is an emplacement for two 90-millimeter (mm) guns. There were also two mobile 90mm guns here as well. The emplacement was an anti-motor torpedo boat defense. This battery had searchlights and a radar tower, now down. The guns of this battery were removed to Fort Monroe in 1975, and were the last remaining guns on the island. Magazine entrances had been filling with sand in 1994, and sand had encroached on the gun emplacements. The Plotting Station was to the northeast of Battery 24, and some fittings from this room still exist. Battery Control, perhaps the plotting station, was the command post for Fort John Custis in 1945. Elements of the Fisherman Island defenses were maintained and garrisoned into 1949.

■ Mine Casemate 4 is a reinforced concrete structure from which submerged mines would have been fired, had they been needed. All the towers related to this structure were demolished under Service ownership. In addition, Sand was covering the access to the interior of the Casemate in 1994, and most of the interior was not visible. Cables protruding from the top of the structure mean that the Casemate may have been reused by the Air Force for a communications related purpose.

These structures may be eligible for the National Register as part of a multi-property nomination of World War II coastal defense structures. In addition, there may be more structures which have been buried by sand.

During the 19th century, the emerging parts of what is today Fisherman Island were jointly owned and used for waterfowling, shell fishing, and fishing. Rights to fish or hunt were sometimes rented to waterman and vacationers. Several cabins related to these activities have been built and moved around on the island throughout the 20th century. There is one remaining cabin on Tract 11. This cabin is reported by the Nature Conservancy to have been an Oyster bed watch cabin. The date of construction, and therefore its potential National Register eligibility, are unknown. Should it be 50 years old, we will need to evaluate its eligibility. In addition to the standing cabin, there are two other cabin sites known from our Land Acquisition Records, but not confirmed by survey.

Appendix F

Appendix F:

Compatibility Determinations

Description of Proposed Use: Hunting

Refuge Name: Eastern Shore of Virginia National Wildlife Refuge

Establishing and Acquisition Authority(ies): Eastern Shore of Virginia National Wildlife Refuge (Eastern Shore of Virginia Refuge) was established under 16 U.S. Code 667b, Public Law 80-537, an Act authorizing the transfer of certain real property for wildlife, or other purposes. Additional parcels of land were acquired under the Migratory Bird Conservation Act, 16 U.S.C. 715d.

Refuge Purpose(s):..... particular value in carrying out the national migratory bird management program. 16 U.S.C. 667b (An Act Authorizing the Transfer of Certain Real Property for Wildlife, or other purposes)..... suitable for (1) incidental fish and wildlife-oriented recreational development, (2) the protection of natural resources, (3) the conservation of endangered species or threatened species ..... 16 U.S.C. 460k-1 (Refuge Recreation Act)..... for the development, advancement, management, conservation, and protection of fish and wildlife resources ..... 16 U.S.C. 742f(a)(4) ..... for the benefit of the United States Fish and Wildlife Service, in performing its activities and services. Such acceptance may be subject to the terms of any restrictive or affirmative covenant, or condition of servitude ..... 16 U.S.C. 742f(b)(1) (Fish and Wildlife Act of 1956)

National Wildlife Refuge System Mission: To administer a national network of lands and waters for the conservation, management, and where appropriate, restoration of the fish, wildlife, and plant resources and their habitats within the United States for the benefit of present and future generations of Americans.

Description of Use:

A. What is the Use? Is the use a priority use?
The use is public hunting. Hunting is identified in the National Wildlife Refuge System Improvement Act of 1997 (USFWS 1997) as a priority public use.

B. Where would the use be conducted?
The Eastern Shore of Virginia National Wildlife Refuge has held an annual deer hunt since 1993. Hunting occurs on approximately 185 acres, which are divided into five hunt zones (see Map F-1). Most of the hunt zones consist of deciduous forest, coniferous forest or a mix of the two, as well as some shrub habitat. These habitats support small and large mammals year round and neotropical migratory birds during their spring and fall migrations.

In Alternative B, we propose opening a portion of the newly acquired Wise Point property to deer hunting (see Map F-2). This would add approximately 40 acres to the current 185 acres open to hunting on the refuge. Hunting on this new land would be conducted in the same way as on the acreage currently open to hunting. Habitats on this acreage are similar to habitats on lands currently hunted.

As proposed in Alternative B we would also open a portion of the newly acquired Wise Point property to waterfowl hunting. The area proposed for opening to waterfowl hunting is approximately 135 acres (see Map F-2). The area is comprised of tidal marsh bisected by extensive tidal creeks and channels. This area supports waterfowl and wading birds, and provides habitat for finfish and shellfish.

C. When would the use be conducted?
Refuge hunts would be conducted during the State big game and waterfowl hunting seasons and would be in accordance with Federal and State regulations. To minimize disturbance to neotropical migrants, hunting with guns would commence in late fall (late November and December). Waterfowl hunting would

adhere to state regulations for bag limits, species, and methods of taking.

How would the use be conducted?

The deer hunt would accommodate a maximum of 23 hunters per day. It is 12 days long with hunting from Monday through Saturday for two consecutive weeks. The archery hunt generally starts at the end of October and extends into November. The shotgun season is seven days long with hunting on Wednesdays and Saturdays in November and December. Both hunts fall within the parameters of the State hunting seasons. Refuge trails and access through the refuge remain open to the public during the archery hunt, but not during the shotgun hunt. The Visitor Center, refuge headquarters and photo blind are the only facilities open during the shotgun hunt. The hunt program achieves the biological objective of reducing the density of the white-tailed deer population.

In Alternative B, we propose to work with the State to modify the deer hunt program to further reduce the deer population because refuge staff have observed heavy browsing in many areas. Taking more deer would further reduce the browse effects on vegetation. This would enable the forest understory to grow and produce more food and cover for neotropical migrants. It would also provide additional food and cover for species such as small mammals, reptiles and invertebrates.

Waterfowl hunting would be allowed by boat only, and only in the area that lies to the southeast of the Virginia Inside Passage (see Map F-2). Waterfowl hunt season dates and bag limits would fall within the parameters of the State's waterfowl season and would be administered in a way that would cause the least disturbance to neotropical migratory birds. This may mean starting the season in December, which would also mitigate conflicts between waterfowl hunting and other wildlife-dependent recreational activities.

Why is the use being proposed?

The refuge deer hunt achieves the biological objective of reducing the density of the white-tailed deer population. High densities of white-tailed deer populations can cause serious habitat degradation by heavily browsing on forest understory and shrubs. Heavily browsed vegetation leaves less food and cover habitat for migratory birds, a trust resource which the refuge is charged with protecting. A controlled refuge hunt would help keep the deer population within the carrying capacity of the habitat.

Waterfowl hunting would helps achieve refuge purposes and management goals and objectives, as outlined in the Comprehensive Conservation Plan (CCP). In addition, waterfowl hunting in these areas is an historic, traditional sustainable activity. Much of the marsh area on the Eastern Shore of Virginia is owned by the State and is already open to migratory bird hunting.

Availability of Resources: Below is a list of costs required to administer and manage the deer hunt on Eastern Shore of Virginia Refuge. We predict opening an additional 40 acres to the deer hunt would not effect these costs.

Refuge Personnel = 1/2 per hunt day @ $100	= $1,900
Dispensing Information during year	= $1,525
Hunter selection/lottery drawing	= $100
Hunter notification/mailing, etc.	= $300
Hunter brochure (design, printing)	= $1,475
Permits/regulations/forms	= $600
Take down signs/closing and moving check station	= $100

Grand total estimated for hunt costs = $6,000

A permit fee of $15 per participant has been collected to defray the cost of the deer hunt. The refuge has had an average of 127 hunters over the past three years, adding up to an average of $1,905 collected in permit fees. Therefore, the total net cost of the hunt is $4,095 ($6,000 - $1,905). In Alternative B of the Draft Comprehensive Conservation Plan/Environmental Assessment (Draft CCP/EA), we propose to double permit costs in order to recover more of our operating costs. The permit fee would increase to $30 per participant (for all hunts conducted at both the Eastern Shore of Virginia and Fisherman Island Refuges).

Funds required to administer and manage waterfowl hunting activities would be similar to or less than deer hunting, depending on how many days we allow hunters to hunt. Below are estimated costs for administering a waterfowl hunt:

Refuge Personnel = 1/2 per hunt day @ $100	= $1,900
Dispensing Information during year	= $1,525
Permits/regulations/forms	= $600
Take down signs	= $100

Total estimated for waterfowl hunt costs = $4,125

Anticipated Impacts of this use: Habitats subject to deer damage include forest understory and shrub habitat that migratory songbirds depend on for food resources. Controlled deer hunting helps keep the deer population within the carrying capacity of the habitat. Heavily browsed vegetation leaves less food and cover habitat for neotropical migratory birds, a trust resource which the refuge is charged with protecting. Modifying the hunt program to further reduce the deer population would then reduce the browse effects on vegetation. This would enable the forest understory to grow and produce more food and cover for neotropical migrants. It would also provide additional food and cover for species such as small mammals, reptiles and invertebrates.

Some wildlife disturbance and trampling of vegetation would occur from deer hunters walking around in their zones. During the shotgun hunt, refuge trails and most of the road system are closed to public use. This causes some conflicts with other users. Shotgun noise from hunting could cause some wildlife disturbance.

Opening a portion of the Wise Point area to waterfowl hunting would have short term impacts on the population that has traditionally used the area for resting and feeding. We predict, however, there will be few long-term impacts on waterfowl populations in this area because few waterfowl use the inland marsh of the Wise Point area (Costanzo 2001). Although we may see an initial rush of hunters who are curious about the area, interest in hunting on the property would probably wane after the first couple years. Furthermore, the property would only accommodate five to 10 hunters. Opening 135 acres to waterfowl hunting would have few cumulative impacts since most of the marsh area on the Eastern Shore of Virginia is owned by the State and is already open to migratory bird hunting.

Hunting provides game meat and recreation for hunters. Hunters who come from outside the local area also contribute to the local economy by staying at local hotels and eating in local restaurants. Providing waterfowl and deer hunting opportunities helps preserve the cultural heritage of the eastern shore of Virginia, where people have hunted and fished for generations.

Public Review and Comments: As part of the CCP process for Eastern Shore of Virginia Refuge, this compatibility determination will undergo extensive public review, including a comment period of 45 days following the release of the Draft CCP/EA.

Determination (check below):

_____ Use is Not Compatible

__X__ Use is Compatible With Following Stipulations

Stipulations to insure compatibility: The hunt program would be managed in accordance with Federal and State regulations. The deer hunt would be reviewed annually to ensure deer management goals are achieved. Both the deer and waterfowl hunts would be reviewed annually to ensure the program is providing a safe, high quality hunting experience for participants. Hunt season dates, bag limits and/or number of hunters per day would be adjusted as needed to achieve balanced wildlife population levels within carrying capacities.

To mitigate user conflicts that arise when we close the refuge to other public uses during shotgun season for deer, we would issue news releases and post information at the Visitor Center to notify visitors of closings.

We maintain a safe deer hunt by limiting the number of hunters per zone and by establishing a buffer zone around refuge residences. We would maintain a safe waterfowl hunt by establishing a buffer zone by the boat ramp to ensure the safety of recreational anglers and commercial watermen using the ramp.

To minimize disturbance to migratory birds in the fall, we would conduct the waterfowl hunt after most birds have migrated (i.e., after November). A later hunt would also limit conflicts with other recreational users. During the hunt season, we would provide a law enforcement presence to insure safety and compliance.

Justification: Hunting is identified in the National Wildlife Refuge System Improvement Act of 1997 as a priority public use. Hunting deer on Eastern Shore of Virginia Refuge is not expected to adversely impact the targeted species because, as apparent from staff observations of deer browsing, we believe there is an overpopulation of deer. Public hunting on Eastern Shore of Refuge would not interfere with nor detract from the fulfillment of the National Wildlife Refuge System mission or the purposes of the Refuge.

Signature: Refuge Manager: _____
(Signature and Date)

Concurrence: Regional Chief: _____
(Signature and Date)

Mandatory 10- or 15-year Re-evaluation Date: _____

Map F-1

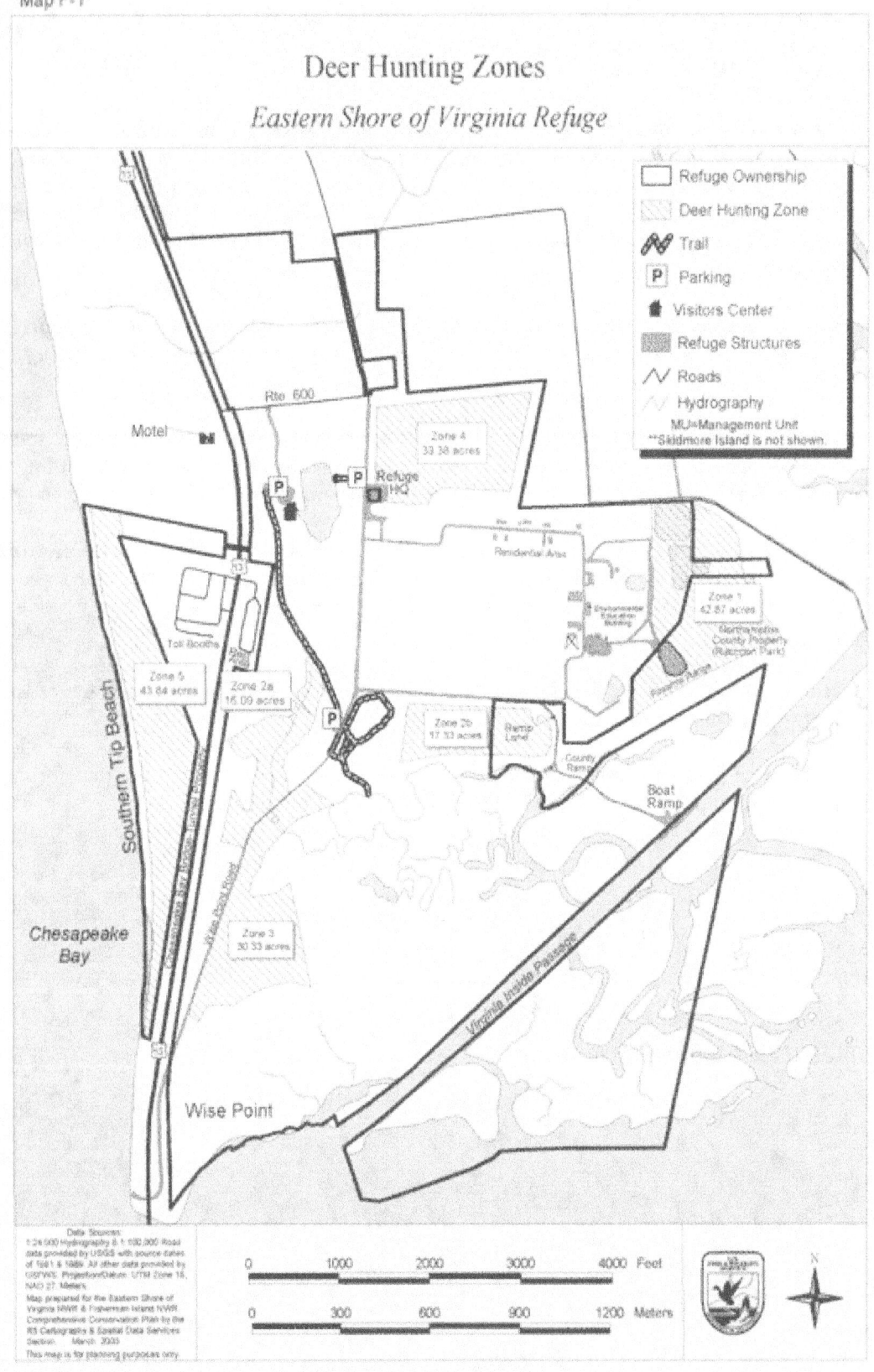

F-6

Alternative B
Proposed Public Use Opportunities
Eastern Shore of Virginia Refuge

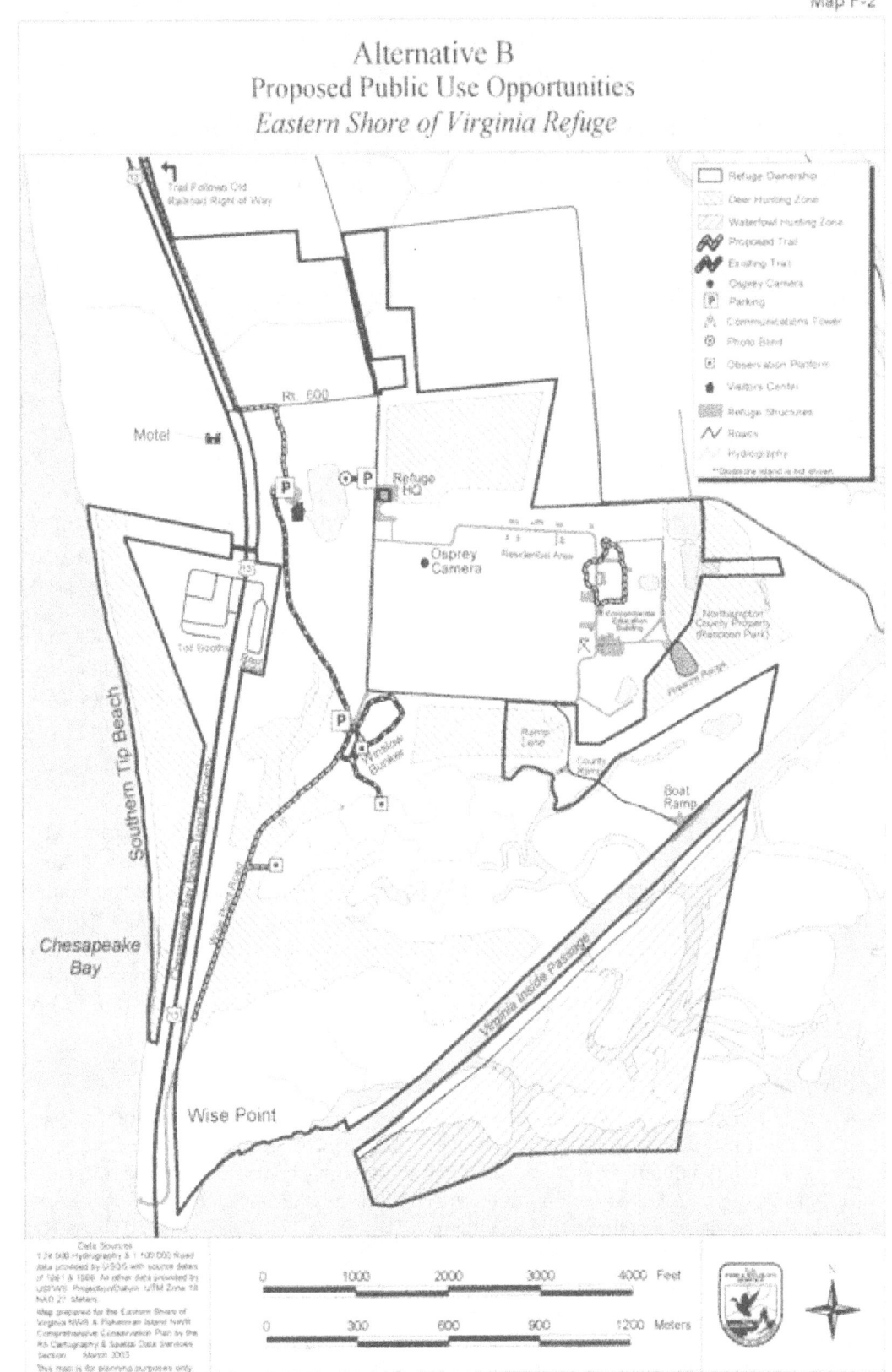

F-7

USE: Commercial and Recreational Boat Access and Commercial Boat Docking at the Wise Point boat ramp.

REFUGE NAME: Eastern Shore of Virginia National Wildlife Refuge

Establishing Authority: Eastern Shore of Virginia National Wildlife Refuge (Eastern Shore of Virginia Refuge) was established under 16 U.S. Code 667b, Public Law 80-537, an Act authorizing the transfer of certain real property for wildlife, or other purposes. Additional parcels of land were acquired under the Migratory Bird Conservation Act, 16 U.S.C. 715d.

Refuge purpose(s): ..... particular value in carrying out the national migratory bird management program. 16 U.S.C. 667b (An Act Authorizing the Transfer of Certain Real Property for Wildlife, or other purposes)

....suitable for (1) incidental fish and wildlife-oriented recreational development, (2) the protection of natural resources, (3) the conservation of endangered species or threatened species ..... 16 U.S.C. 460k-1 (Refuge Recreation Act)

..... for the development, advancement, management, conservation, and protection of fish and wildlife resources ..... 16 U.S.C. 742f(a)(4) ..... for the benefit of the United States Fish and Wildlife Service, in performing its activities and services. Such acceptance may be subject to the terms of any restrictive or affirmative covenant, or condition of servitude ..... 16 U.S.C. 742f(b)(1) (Fish and Wildlife Act of 1956)

National Wildlife Refuge System Mission: To administer a national network of lands and waters for the conservation, management, and where appropriate, restoration of the fish, wildlife, and plant resources and their habitats within the United States for the benefit of present and future generations of Americans.

Description of use:

(a) What is the use? Is the use a priority public use?
Recreational and commercial boat access and historically permitted commercial boat docking (must meet certain criteria) at the Wise Point boat ramp. Recreational and commercial fishermen and recreational boaters have requested use of the Wise Point boat ramp to gain access to fishing and hunting grounds on both the Atlantic Ocean and Chesapeake Bay. Commercial watermen that historically docked at Wise Point are requesting continued overnight docking privileges. Recreational and commercial boat access and commercial boat docking are not identified in the National Wildlife Refuge System Improvement Act of 1997 (USFWS 1997) as priority public uses.

(b) Where would the use be conducted?
The Wise Point boat ramp is located at the terminus of Ramp Lane (see Map F-3) and adjacent to the deep waters of the Virginia Inside Passage. The facilities and access to this site include approximately15 acres of tidally influenced salt marsh, maritime forest, shrub thickets and a dredge spoil site. Other areas that would be affected incidental to use include the barrier islands and extensive tidal marshes along the southern terminus of the Delmarva Peninsula [e.g., Fisherman Island Refuge, Skidmore Island (Service ownership); Smith, Myrtle and Ship Shoal Islands (The Nature Conservancy ownership); Mockhorn Island (State Wildlife Management Area)]. These barrier islands and tidal marshes are one of the only remaining undeveloped barrier systems in the mid-Atlantic region. Their extensive coastal salt marshes, bays, barrier beaches and interdunal ponds provide high value migration, wintering and breeding habitat for extensive numbers and variety of colonial nesting waterbirds and wading birds, migrating and wintering waterfowl and migrating neotropical songbirds. The barrier/

marsh system has been identified as a priority for protection in the North American Waterfowl Management Plan: Atlantic Coast Joint Venture (USFWS 1988) and as a United Nations Biosphere Reserve. The islands have been designated as a Western Hemisphere Shorebird Reserve Network of international importance.

(c) When would the use be conducted?

The Wise Point boat ramp would be open daily to recreational anglers and boaters and commercial watermen during normal refuge hours (½ hour before sunrise to ½ hour after sunset) with extended hours during certain seasons. The ramp would be open for 24-hour access to a limited number of permitted commercial watermen that were using the area on a commercial basis and paying a commercial rate at the time of U.S. Fish and Wildlife Service (Service) purchase (12/26/2001). The refuge may be closed at certain times (e.g., gun hunt, prescribed burning), thus impacting access to the boat ramp at those times.

(d) How would the use be conducted?

The entrance road would be improved and widened (in certain areas) to allow for vehicles to safely pass each other. Also, the parking lot would be improved and enlarged (in areas that are upland and presently maintained by mowing) and a boat ramp, commercial dock and commercial off-loading site would be constructed. Supporting facilities would include restrooms, lighting, an electric gate, overflow/satellite parking and signing (interpretive, regulatory and directional).

After improvements have been completed and the area is safe for general use a concessionaire would be contracted to manage the site. If an acceptable concessionaire is not found management would be through the refuge fee program.

(e) Why is this use being proposed?

The Wise Point boat ramp is located on the deep waters of the Virginia Inside Passage which was constructed in the 1950's and bisects the refuge. Despite miles of shoreline in Northampton County, public deep water access is limited. There are six public boat access points in Northampton County (not including Wise Point), with the closest ramp on the Atlantic Ocean located 10 miles north in Oyster. On the Chesapeake Bay the closest public ramp is 3.5 miles away, at Kiptopeke State Park. Both of these ramps are used beyond capacity during certain summer days and other popular fishing times. Additionally, the Wise Point site is ideal because of its proximity to the Chesapeake Bay Bridge Tunnel, a popular fishing location. The ramp location also affords a relatively safe harbor because of the islands and marshes to the east which provide protection to boaters during storms and high winds.

There was limited historic use by both recreational and commercial users before the area became part of the Eastern Shore of Virginia Refuge. Because of both the demand and limited suitable sites for boat launching in the county, there is an expectation that this site be available to the public. Additionally, there were 21 commercial watermen paying for and using this site on a commercial basis. Many of these commercial watermen have Commonwealth-leased grounds and permits for locations in close proximity to the Wise Point ramp. These watermen have a vested interest in gaining access that is proximate to their established work sites. Northampton County, which has little revenue from industrial and manufacturing businesses, is trying to balance maintaining the rural atmosphere of the County and their fiscal needs. The Wise Point boat ramp will bring dollars to the County through use by recreational boaters, ecotourism and commercial watermen in the form of job opportunities, taxation on commercial catch, and purchase of fuel, food and lodging. Thus, the Service would be a partner with the County in maintaining the area with these rural qualities.

Availability of Resources:

Improvements to the boat ramp and associated facilities are included in the Service's Maintenance Management System (MMS) database (51650-02003, $445,000) and are estimated as follows:

Boat ramp.. $55,000 (2-lane concrete base)
Bulkhead.. $196,000
Courtesy tie-off.. $54,000
Commercial dock and mooring.................. $104,000
Contracting, permits and miscellaneous.... $36,000

The entrance road and parking lot improvements and associated facilities are part of a Federal Highway TEA-21 project and are estimated as follows:

Entrance road upgrade............................... $250,000
Pull offs.. $35,000
Parking area improvements and enlargement........... $60,000
Satellite parking development................................ $10,000
Restrooms, lighting and fee station......................... $20,000
Electric gate and signs.. $20,000
Interpretive and regulatory signs............................ $5,000

Additional one-time costs that would not be covered by TEA-21 are :

Purchase two vehicles $40,000
Upgrade environmental education building as offices...........$35,000

The total estimated construction and upgrade costs are $920,000.

Daily and annual fee structures would be offered for recreational boaters. Day-use permits would cost $10 and an annual pass would cost $120 (rates would change over time). Users who were commercially using the area and paying a commercial rate when the Service purchased the site would pay an annual fee of $1,500 for those who dock their boats and $600 for those who do not dock their boats (no new docking privileges will be granted). New commercial users and commercial users that were not paying a commercial fee when the Service purchased the property would be allowed to use the site commercially and would be charged $400 annually. These new commercial users would not be granted use of the docks, reserved parking, nor 24 hour, seven days a week access. However, they would be allowed to use the unloading area for commercial catch.

If a concessionaire is contracted, it would be responsible for selling passes and ensuring the smooth and orderly operation of the boat ramp. Under this scenario one full-time and two seasonal Law Enforcement Officers would be hired (2.08 FTEs) and administrative, management and maintenance time would be needed to manage the site. Additionally, there would be added expenses for annual maintenance and fuel and energy costs. The estimated annual costs for this option is delineated below. If the ramp is managed as a refuge fee program, an additional seasonal Law Enforcement Officer, two fee collectors and additional oversight would be needed by refuge staff.

Annual refuge costs for the upkeep and administration of the recreational and commercial boat access and commercial boat docking at the Wise Point boat ramp under a concessionaire includes:

Full-time LE Officer (GS-7/9) $64,000
Seasonal LE Officer (0.66 FTE) (GS-5) $21,000
Seasonal LE Officer (0.42 FTE) (GS-4) $13,000

Administrative oversight ....$ 7,000
Fuel and energy costs ....$ 4,000
Road and parking lot upkeep (grading and aggregate).........$12,000
Maintenance of electric gate ....$ 2,000
Dumpster contract ....$ 1,000
Restroom maintenance ....$ 1,500
Brochures, annual permit tags, sign maintenance.................$ 2,500

Annual Boat Ramp Costs..$128,000

Under the concessionaire scenario, entrance and user fees would go to the concessionaire to defray the costs of managing the boat ramp. Therefore, the annual costs for managing the boat ramp, from the Service's perspective, would come from budget allocations. The information below shows funding received in fiscal year 2002. Additional funding would be required to manage this ramp in a safe and orderly manner.

FY 02 Budget Allocation included:
　　　Salaries...$414,500
　　　Fixed Costs.................................$ 28,400
　　　Station Base Funds......................$ 9,400
　　　Base Maintenance.......................$ 17,800

　　　Total Available Funds.................$470,100

Presuming fiscal year 2003 and subsequent base budgets are increased by 27 percent over fiscal year 2002, funding would be adequate to ensure compatibility and to administer and manage the recreational use listed.

Anticipated Impacts of the Use: Once improvements are complete and the area is reopened to recreational boaters, there would be increased ramp usage and increased boat traffic in the surrounding waters. This increase would cause wildlife disturbance and would have an impact on water quality (both from turbidity and increased oil and gas). The Wise Point ramp would also give boaters easy access to a number of sensitive barrier islands and saltwater marshes. The barrier islands have large numbers of beach nesting (e.g., American oystercatcher) and colonial nesting (e.g., royal tern) birds that would be adversely impacted by noise, human presence, pets and litter. The concern is that nesting pairs and whole colonies could be lost if human disturbance is not controlled. Additionally, there is a concern that litter could increase the gull population, which could cause increased predation on the colonial and beach nesting birds and eggs. It is during the warm nesting season that the largest number of boaters are likely to be using the ramp and have an interest in accessing nearby beaches for strolling, shell collecting, picnics and rest breaks.

Marsh birds (e.g., black ducks, tri-colored herons, snowy egrets) would also be adversely impacted by boaters navigating the marshes. These impacts would include human presence, pets (i.e., running or barking dogs), engine noise and boat wakes.

Improvements to the boat ramp would cause some one-time disturbances to biological resources. Boat ramp and dock construction and installing mooring posts would require dredging and pumping, which would cause some temporary water turbidity. Additionally, dredging and pier/ mooring post removal may bring some previously submerged contaminants (e.g., oil, DDT) to the surface.

Installation of a culvert(s) under Ramp Lane would alter the hydrology of the impoundment. This impoundment was historically a tidally-influenced salt marsh, which was impounded by creation of the road that essentially cut the marsh off from cyclic tides. Installing a culvert(s) would improve the hydrology and assist in reverting this area to salt marsh. With the daily flushing of salt water, the invasive phragmites that rings the impoundment would also be adversely impacted, and *spartina* and other salt marsh vegetation would return. However, because of siltation and other changes that have occurred since this area was impounded, it would not immediately be the same quality marsh it once was.

Adding pull-offs to Ramp Lane to enhance driving safety would require some filling of salt marsh and cutting of vegetation along the upland areas of the road. Although engineering specifications have not been completed it is estimated that approximately one-third of an acre of wetlands would be filled and one-half acre of uplands would be cleared for pull-offs. Additionally, approximately one-half acre of uplands would be cleared for a satellite parking area.

Grading and graveling the entrance road and parking lot would cause some siltation in adjacent waters. This would cause water turbidity affecting wetland vegetation, benthic organisms and fisheries.

An electric gate would be installed which would require trenching to run electricity to the gate and installation of a magnetic plate under the road surface.

Finally, the Eastern Shore of Virginia Refuge would experience an increase in traffic within its boundaries which would cause wildlife disturbance and may also increase litter and vandalism.

Public review and comment: As part of the Comprehensive Conservation Planning (CCP) process for Eastern Shore of Virginia Refuge, this compatibility determination will undergo extensive public review, including a comment period of 45 days following the release of the Draft Comprehensive Conservation Plan/Environmental Assessment (Draft CCP/EA).

Determination (check below):

_____ **Use is Not Compatibility**

__X__ **Use is Compatible With Following Stipulations**

Stipulations to ensure compatibility: To reduce wildlife disturbance on nearby barrier islands no pets would be allowed in the boat ramp area (thereby not allowing any pets on boats). Additionally, no personal watercrafts (PWCs) would be allowed on the Eastern Shore of Virginia Refuge. Denying PWC access through this boat ramp would reduce the noise, wake and disturbance that these watercrafts often cause. Large closed area signs would be installed on the refuge barrier islands to inform boaters these areas are off-limits to foot access and boat landing. Law enforcement staff would be hired to patrol Skidmore Island and Fisherman Island Refuges. Law enforcement patrols would minimize the number of boaters illegally landing on these refuges. Additionally, law enforcement would discourage vandalism, litter and other illegal activities, as well as help ensure smooth management of the boat ramp area.

Parking for this boat ramp (total combined spaces at the ramp and satellite parking) would be capped at 75 parking spaces. Increasing boat access beyond this level may adversely affect the sensitive wildlife resources within Eastern Shore of Virginia Refuge and the surrounding barrier islands and marshes that harbor large numbers of migratory and resident birds and also provide a nursery for the abundant fisheries resources in this area.

An environmentally sound human waste disposal system (e.g., composting toilets) would be used. Solar lighting, with down-shielded lights, would also be used. No water or electricity service would be run to the site and no fish cleaning would be allowed on-site, thereby reducing the amount of food available to gulls, raccoons and other predators. An interpretive sign installed at the boat ramp would explain the sensitivity of the barrier islands and marshes and how boaters can minimize human disturbance. A training course would be developed for commercial tour guides (e.g., kayak tours) and all tour guides would be required to take a training course before taking trips from the Wise Point boat ramp. The course would focus on minimizing human disturbance to wildlife resources on barrier islands and marsh areas.

Speed bumps would be placed along the entrance to minimize vehicle speeds and a system would be designed to inform the boating public when the parking areas are full, prior to arriving at the launch site. This would reduce the number of vehicles entering when there is no parking available. Both of these details would reduce wildlife disturbance on the Eastern Shore of Virginia Refuge.

Boat docking would be phased out over time. Since the boat dock and mooring posts are in direct and sole support of a commercial use, it cannot be justified on a national wildlife refuge. Once the commercial watermen (those that met certain criteria when the land was purchased) retire or terminate commercial fishing from this site their docking rights will be relinquished. However, their other special rights (24-hour access, set aside parking) may be passed on to one heir (after the second generation all special rights will be terminated). This heir has to be a named individual (not a business) and must actively participate in commercial fisheries from this site.

We would partner with the Commonwealth to extend the no-wake zone in the Virginia Inside Passage, adjacent to refuge property. This would decrease turbidity and disturbance from increased boat usage. Baseline water quality and sediment surveys would be conducted and bi-annual surveys would be performed to determine the impacts of increased boat usage on biotic and abiotic elements. To prevent fill used for grading the entrance road and parking lot from eroding into the water, silt fencing would be used during construction.

Justification: Eastern Shore of Virginia Refuge was established under provisions of the national migratory bird management program. In addition, tracts were purchased under the authorities of the Migratory Bird Conservation Act of 1929, as amended, which pertains to the acquisition, development, and maintenance of migratory bird refuges. This use has been determined to be compatible given that it would be managed at a level and in a manner that does not result in hazards to visitors, unresolvable conflicts between user groups, nor significant habitat degradation or wildlife disturbance, and provided that the stipulations referenced are implemented. This use would not materially interfere with or detract from the mission of the National Wildlife Refuge System or the purposes for which the refuge was established. This use would not pose adverse effects on trust species or other refuge resources and would not interfere with other uses being conducted on the refuge.

Signature: Refuge   Manager: _____
                                          (Signature and Date)

Concurrence: Regional Chief: _____
                                          (Signature and Date)

Mandatory 10- or 15-year Re-evaluation Date: _____

Map F-3

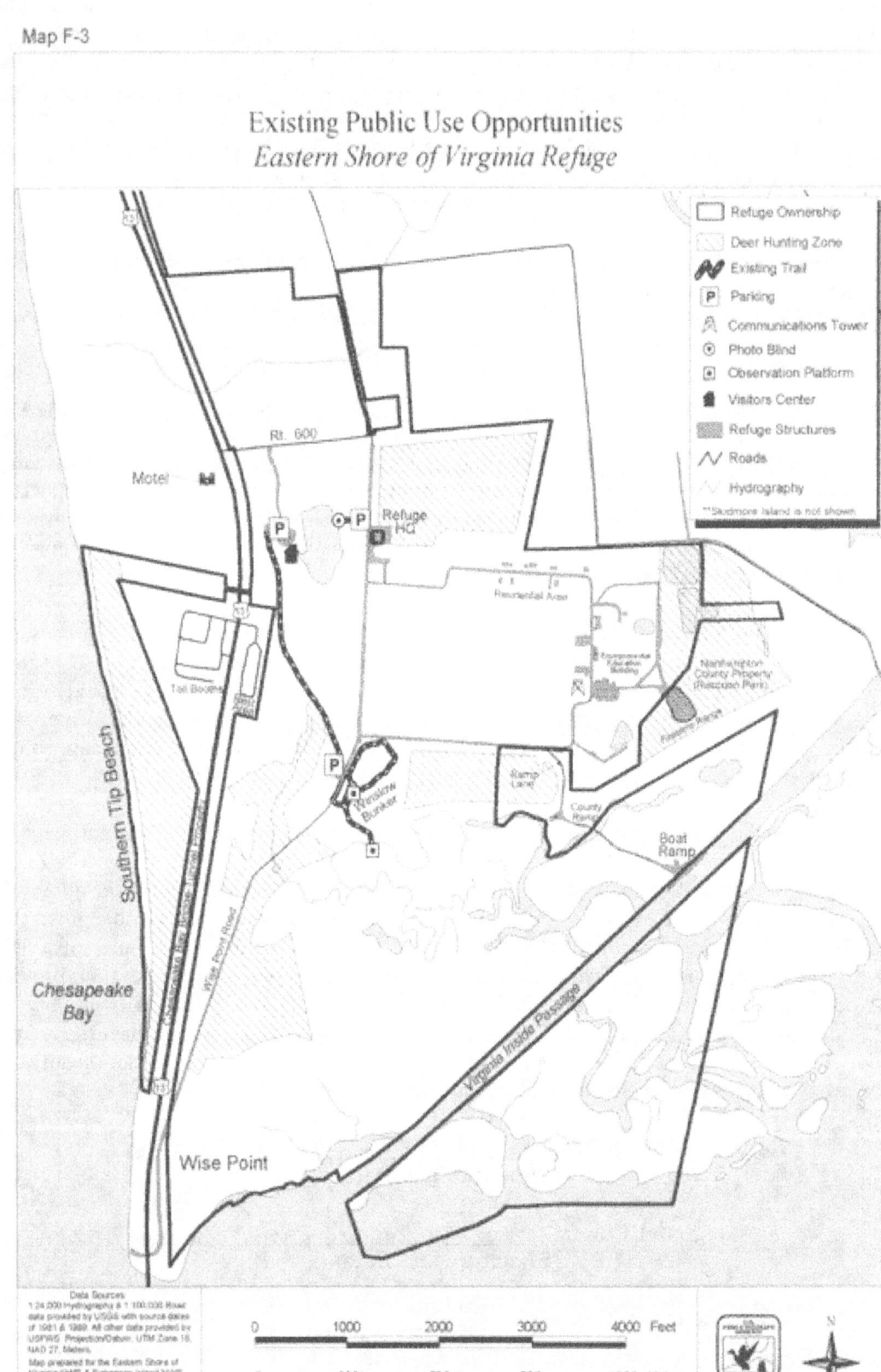

Existing Public Use Opportunities
Eastern Shore of Virginia Refuge

	Refuge Ownership
	Deer Hunting Zone
	Existing Trail
	Parking
	Communications Tower
	Photo Blind
	Observation Platform
	Visitors Center
	Refuge Structures
	Roads
	Hydrography

**Skidmore Island is not shown

Rt. 600

Motel

Refuge HQ

Residential Area

Environmental Education Building

Northampton County Property (Raccoon Park)

Southern Tip Beach

Toll Booths

Western Bunker

Ramp Lane

County Ramp

Boat Ramp

Chesapeake Bay

Wise Point

Virginia Inside Passage

Data Sources
1:24,000 Hydrography & 1:100,000 Road
data provided by USGS with source dates
of 1981 & 1989. All other data provided by
USFWS. Projection/Datum: UTM Zone 18,
NAD 27, Meters.
Map prepared for the Eastern Shore of
Virginia NWR & Fisherman Island NWR
Comprehensive Conservation Plan by the
R5 Cartography & Spatial Data Services
Section   March 2003
This map is for planning purposes only.

| 0 | 1000 | 2000 | 3000 | 4000 Feet |

| 0 | 300 | 600 | 900 | 1200 Meters |

N

F-14

Use: Wildlife Observation, Wildlife Photography, Interpretation and Environmental Education

Refuge Name: Eastern Shore of Virginia National Wildlife Refuge

Establishing and Acquisition Authority(ies): Eastern Shore of Virginia National Wildlife Refuge (Eastern Shore of Virginia Refuge) was established under 16 U.S. Code 667b, Public Law 80-537, an Act authorizing the transfer of certain real property for wildlife, or other purposes. Additional parcels of land were acquired under the Migratory Bird Conservation Act, 16 U.S.C. 715d.

Refuge Purpose(s): ..... particular value in carrying out the national migratory bird management program. 16 U.S.C. 667b (An Act Authorizing the Transfer of Certain Real Property for Wildlife, or other purposes)..... suitable for (1) incidental fish and wildlife-oriented recreational development, (2) the protection of natural resources, (3) the conservation of endangered species or threatened species ..... 16 U.S.C. 460k-1 (Refuge Recreation Act)..... for the development, advancement, management, conservation, and protection of fish and wildlife resources ..... 16 U.S.C. 742f(a)(4) ..... for the benefit of the United States Fish and Wildlife Service, in performing its activities and services. Such acceptance may be subject to the terms of any restrictive or affirmative covenant, or condition of servitude ..... 16 U.S.C. 742f(b)(1) (Fish and Wildlife Act of 1956)

National Wildlife Refuge System Mission: To administer a national network of lands and waters for the conservation, management, and where appropriate, restoration of the fish, wildlife, and plant resources and their habitats within the United States for the benefit of present and future generations of Americans.

Description of Use:

A. What is the use? Is the use a priority use?
The uses are wildlife observation, wildlife photography, environmental education and interpretation. These uses are priority public uses, as identified in the National Wildlife Refuge Improvement Act (USFWS 1997).

B. Where would the use be conducted?

All uses are conducted on Eastern Shore of Virginia Refuge within regular refuge hours, which are a half-hour before sunrise to a half-hour after sunset. A 1.5-mile trail system from the Visitor Center to the Winslow Bunker offers year-round opportunities for observing neotropical migratory species such as birds and butterflies. Two overlooks along the trail -- one on top of the Winslow Bunker and another at the edge of a salt marsh -- provide opportunities for viewing migrating birds overhead and wading birds such as herons and egrets at the marsh's edge. An observation window in the Visitor Center overlooks a freshwater pond with a variety of duck species.

C. When would the use be conducted?
All uses would be conducted within regular refuge hours, which are a half-hour before sunrise to a half-hour after sunset.

D. How would the use be conducted?
A photo blind opposite the refuge headquarters offers opportunities for wildlife photography, as does the 1.5-mile trail system and its two overlooks. The staff conducts educational programs and guided interpretive walks for over 6,000 people each year and an additional 45,000 people participate in self-guided activities and non-staff conducted educational programs. On Eastern Shore of Virginia Refuge, these activities occur along trails and in the Visitor Center. Refuge staff visit local schools and hold several events on the refuge, such as birding festivals. Interpretive signs along the refuge's trail system

offer opportunities for environmental interpretation. For a complete list of all current activities associated with wildlife observation, wildlife photography, environmental education and interpretation, see Alternative A, Goal 4.

Alternative B (the Proposed Action) would continue with the above uses and add the following to improve the educational and interpretive programs for the public.

■   Design and construct an environmental study area to include a half-mile trail, three teaching stations and a pavilion. Remodel the environmental education building to include a wet lab, indoor classrooms, hands-on exhibits and a teacher resource library.

■   Develop new Visitor Center exhibits including a diorama and video segment.

■   Replace Visitor Center exhibits.

■   Enhance environmental education programs.

■   Develop a three-mile bike trail along an old railroad right-of way that runs parallel to U.S. Route 13. The trail would include two interpretive exhibit panels on migratory birds and their habitat.

■   Open .6 miles of the Wise Point Road to foot traffic and construct a 200-foot boardwalk that leads to a marsh overlook. The boardwalk would end in an observation platform measuring 16 feet x 19 feet, with an interpretive panel.

■   Hire a recreational assistant to help develop new interpretive displays, outreach exhibits, educational lesson plans, annual teacher's workshops, photography workshops and monthly educational programs. (Proposed RONS project)

E. Why is the use being proposed?

Wildlife observation, wildlife photography, environmental education, and interpretation are priority public uses as defined by The National Wildlife Refuge System Administration Act of 1966, as amended by the National Wildlife Refuge System Improvement Act of 1997 (Public Law 105-57), and if compatible, are to receive enhanced consideration over other general public uses.

Availability of Resources: Most of the projects below are already included in the Service's Maintenance Management System (MMS) or Refuge Operations Needs System (RONS) database for funding. Some projects, under Alternative B, have been proposed for inclusion in one of these two databases. For a complete list of current and proposed MMS and RONS databases, see Appendix G.

•   Design and construct an environmental study area to include a half-mile trail, three teaching stations and a pavilion. Remodel the environmental education building to include a wet lab, indoor classrooms, hands-on exhibits and a teacher resource library. (MMS Project #00003)

        Cost Estimate = $42,000

•   Develop new Visitor Center exhibits including a diorama and video segment;
    (RONS project #93111)

            FTE's = 0

            Equipment costs: $32,000

            Services/Supplies: $30,000

            Miscellaneous:$3,000

            Total Cost: $65,000

•   Replace Visitor Center exhibits (MMS project #98507)

        Cost Estimate = $125,000

•   Enhance environmental education programs. (RONS project #93107)

            FTE's =   0

            Equipment costs: $34,000

            Facilities costs: $48,000

Services/Supplies: $4,000 first year, $4,000 recurring

Miscellaneous: $10,000 first year, $2,000 recurring

Total Cost: $102,000

•   Develop a three-mile bike trail along an old railroad right-of way that runs parallel to U.S. Route 13. The trail would include two interpretive exhibit panels on migratory birds and their habitat. (RONS project #00009)

FTEs   =   0

First-year cost = $44,000

Recurring costs = $6,000

Project duration = 2 years

•   Open .6 miles of the Wise Point Road to foot traffic and construct a 200-foot boardwalk that leads to a marsh overlook. The boardwalk will end in an observation platform measuring 16 feet x 19 feet, with an interpretive panel.

(Proposed RONS project)

FTE's = 0

First-year cost = $22,000

Recurring costs = $3,000

Project duration = 2 years

•   Hire a recreational assistant to help develop new interpretive displays, outreach exhibits, educational lesson plans, annual teacher's workshops, photography workshops and monthly educational programs. (Proposed RONS project)

FTE's = 1 (GS-5)

First-year cost = $40,000 for FTE, $10,000 for materials

Recurring costs = $34,000

Project duration = 15 years

Anticipated Impacts of the Use: We predict impacts from the renovation of the environmental education building would be minimal because we are not constructing a new building. Most of the renovations to the building would be on the inside. The only new construction would be the trail and the pavilion located along the trail. Any construction in this area would cause minimal disturbance because it is already a disturbed area. The site of the proposed trail is also in a disturbed area, except for a portion of the trail that would run through a small amount of forest habitat (50-100 feet). Adding a trail would require mowing a strip of land and possibly laying down gravel in some areas. This would impact vegetation, causing some soil compaction which ultimately reduces vegetation composition and structure. Construction of the boardwalk would create a one-time disturbance to a portion of the pond bottom by installing posts. The pond measures about one acre and is shallow. In dry years, there is no standing water. The pond sees occasional water bird use. More birds use the pond to the north, which would not be disturbed by the new trail.

Opening a portion of the Wise Point Road may cause disturbance to neotropical avian species. Some research suggests human intrusion in wildlife habitats, such as walking on trails, can cause disturbance to wildlife. One example is a study (Gutzwiller et. al, 1997) that showed human intrusion influences avian singing behavior in some species. During breeding season, the seasonal timing of male song affects the timing of territory establishments, male attraction, pair formation, egg laying, and transmission of information about breeding songs to young (Gutzwiller, et. al, 1997). Therefore, if human intrusion affects singing, it could ultimately affect reproduction and survival of some species. Another study (Riffell et. al, 1996) suggests that when repeated human intrusion recurs over an extended period of time, impacts on avian reproductive fitness have the potential to accumulate temporally at the individual, population and community levels. However, the refuge's main role in the life cycle of avian species is not during breeding but rather during migration. Also, the Wise Point Road is in an already disturbed area, at 50-100 yards from Route 13, a major four-lane highway.

Constructing the Wise Point Road trail would have minimal impact since there is already a paved road there. We would, however, disturb vegetation to create a 200-foot boardwalk with a platform overlook onto the salt marsh. This may require the taking of a small amount of salt marsh. Providing trails for public use could also result in litter, vandalism, removing plants and/or animals, and trespassing into closed areas.

The three-mile bike trail would run along an old railroad right-of-way which is in FWS ownership. The bike trail would measure about eight feet wide; the right-of-way is a total of 66 feet wide. The trail would run north from the refuge, parallel to U.S. Route 13, a major highway, with about 100-150 feet buffering the trail from the road. The east side of the trail would border agricultural land. Given the proximity of the trail to a major highway and to agricultural fields, the wildlife values are reduced. The configuration of the land as a long, thin corridor also makes it less valuable for habitat. Therefore, disturbance to wildlife would be minimal.

Public Review and Comments: As part of the Comprehensive Conservation Plan (CCP) process for Eastern Shore of Virginia Refuge, this compatibility determination will undergo extensive public review, including a comment period of 45 days following the release of the Draft Comprehensive Conservation Plan/Environmental Assessment (Draft CCP/EA).

Determination (check below):

_____ **Use is Not Compatible**

__X__ **Use is Compatible With Following Stipulations**

Stipulations Necessary to Ensure Compatibility: Public use areas would be monitored at various times of the year to assess wildlife disturbance. We would include information about proper etiquette and the effects of human impacts on habitat and wildlife resources in refuge publications and flyers, on kiosks and in interpretive programs discussions. Periodic law enforcement would ensure compliance with regulations and area closures, and would discourage vandalism.

To limit wildlife disturbance, the new environmental education trail would only be used for scheduled outdoor educational activities. This would add up to about twice a day during the spring, once a week during the summer and less in the fall and winter. The area would be monitored throughout the year and, if necessary, trail use would be restricted during certain times to minimize disturbance to wildlife. The boardwalk to the pond would be built over, instead of directly on, wetland vegetation so as to minimize disturbance to vegetation.

We would limit access to the Wise Point Trail by offering only guided tours during the fall migration of neotropical and temperate migrants. This would help minimize disturbance to birds who are feeding and resting during their migration south to wintering habitat. All other times of the year, the trail would be open to visitors during normal refuge hours. If salt marsh is taken or disturbed to build the boardwalk and overlook on the Wise Point Road trail, we would restore an equal amount of salt marsh elsewhere on the refuge.

Justification: One of the secondary goals of the National Wildlife Refuge System is to provide opportunities for the public to develop an understanding and appreciation for wildlife wherever those opportunities are compatible. Environmental education, interpretation, wildlife observation and photography are identified in the National Wildlife Refuge System Improvement Act of 1997 as priority public uses. These activities would not materially interfere with or detract from the fulfillment of the National Wildlife Refuge System mission or the purposes of the refuge.

Signature: **Refuge Manager:** _____

                                             (Signature and Date)

Concurrence: Regional Chief: _____

                                   (Signature and Date)

Mandatory 10- or 15-year Re-evaluation Date: _____

Description of Proposed Use: Archery Hunting for White-tailed Deer

Refuge Name: Fisherman Island National Wildlife Refuge

Establishing and Acquisition Authority(ies): Fisherman Island National Wildlife Refuge (Fisherman Island Refuge) was established under 16 U.S. Code 667b, Public Law 80-537, an Act authorizing the transfer of certain real property for wildlife, or other purposes. An additional parcel of land on the island was acquired under the Migratory Bird Conservation Act, 16 U.S.C. 715d.

Refuge Purpose(s): ..... particular value in carrying out the national migratory bird management program. 16 U.S.C. 667b (An Act Authorizing the Transfer of Certain Real Property for Wildlife, or other purposes)

National Wildlife Refuge System Mission: To administer a national network of lands and waters for the conservation, management, and where appropriate, restoration of the fish, wildlife, and plant resources and their habitats within the United States for the benefit of present and future generations of Americans.

Description of Use:

A. What is the use? Is the use a priority use?
Fisherman Island Refuge will open to a biologically-managed white-tailed deer hunt. Hunting is identified in the National Wildlife Refuge System Improvement Act of 1997 (USFWS 1997) as a priority public use. A management hunt refers to a hunt that is open to the public but is conducted based on biological needs and is not necessarily held annually. Refuge staff will perform habitat surveys for browse damage assessment and will work with State partners to assess the health and size of the white-tailed deer population. These data will be used annually to decide whether to open the refuge to hunting.

B. Where would the use be conducted?
Approximately 75 acres of upland vegetation, adjacent to the unimproved entrance road onto Fisherman Island and north and west of the Chesapeake Bay Bridge Tunnel roadway, would be open to an archery management hunt for white-tailed deer (see Map F-4).

C. When would the use be conducted?
The hunt would be administered during the State big game hunting season and in accordance with State regulations. This archery hunt would be conducted during Eastern Shore of Virginia National Wildlife Refuge's (Eastern Shore of Virginia Refuge's) gun hunt season (conducted in late November and December), to minimize disturbance to neotropical migrants.

D. How would the use be conducted?
Hunting would take place in designated hunt stand locations in the uplands adjacent to the unimproved entrance road on the west side of U.S. Route 13. We would work with the State to determine safe number of hunters for this habitat. However, it is estimated the area would accommodate between 4-6 hunters per day. This archery hunt would follow the same schedule as the Eastern Shore of Virginia Refuge shotgun hunt, typically on Wednesdays and Saturdays for seven days from late November through mid-December. However, hunt days may change if more hunters would participate or if take would be increased with a change of schedule, i.e., having consecutive hunt days may draw more hunters. The hunt days would be consistent with the hunt days at the Eastern Shore of Virginia Refuge. Hunters would bring all harvested deer to the Eastern Shore of Virginia Refuge check station. One deviation of this hunt from the gun hunt is that deer would not be field dressed on Fisherman Island Refuge, rather a site would be provided on the Eastern Shore of Virginia Refuge for hunters that want to field dress their deer before departure. This would be an antlerless deer hunt only.

Safe access onto the island will be described in published annual refuge hunting regulations. All hunters would be required to attend an annual hunter orientation. The hunt program would be reviewed annually to ensure deer management goals are achieved (i.e., the resident white-tailed deer population is being reduced) and that the program is providing a safe, high quality hunting experience for participants.

E. Why is the use being proposed?

Initiating a deer hunt on Fisherman Island Refuge would achieve the biological objective of reducing the density of the white-tailed deer population. High densities of white-tailed deer can cause serious habitat degradation by heavy browsing on forest understory and shrubs. Heavily-browsed vegetation leaves less food and cover habitat for migratory birds, a trust resource which the refuge is charged with protecting. A controlled management hunt may keep the deer population at levels that reduce habitat damage. However, if a public hunt is not successful in meeting these objectives, other management techniques would be considered.

Availability of Resources:

The cost of opening Fisherman Island Refuge to hunting includes the following expenses:

Conducting hunter orientation	$2,000
1 FTE per hunt day @ $150/day	$1,050
Dispensing hunt information	$900
Hunter selection/lottery drawing	$100
Hunter notification/mailing	$150
Hunter brochure (design, printing)	$900
Permits/regulations/forms	$600
Posting hunt area and deer stand locations	$500
Take down signs	$100
Conducting habitat surveys	$1,500
Total	**$7,800**

Some aspects of managing this hunt would be tied into managing the existing hunt on the Eastern Shore of Virginia Refuge. However, additional costs would be incurred since the hunt would be conducted in a geographically distinct area. Some costs would be recouped in permit fees ($630 if all slots were filled). Presently a permit fee of $15 per participant is being collected to defray the cost of the hunt on the Eastern Shore of Virginia Refuge. However, we are only recuperating about 40 percent of the costs of conducting the hunt. Therefore, the hunt permit fee for all hunts conducted at both the Eastern Shore of Virginia and Fisherman Island Refuges would increase to $30 to recover more of our operating costs.

Anticipated Impacts on Service Lands, Waters or Interest:

Opening Fisherman Island Refuge to an archery hunt would help reduce the impacts of deer browse on the island. It would also provide additional food and cover for species such as songbirds, small mammals, reptiles and invertebrates. The hunt would cause some trampling of unstable dunes and vegetation. Damage to vegetation and within these unstable soils and dunes would likely incur when hunters are tracking wounded deer.

Opening Fisherman Island Refuge to a deer hunt could increase the predator population. For instance, if hunters field dressed deer on the island the entrails could attract predators and provide food to improve the health of these predators so that they could better survive the winter months. This is considered a potentially serious problem, as most other barrier islands along the Virginia coastline are plagued with avian predator issues. Because of this potential problem, no field dressing would be allowed on Fisherman Island. Another concern is the potential introduction of invasive plants from hunters walking on the island with boots that may be harboring seeds from invasive plants found on the Eastern Shore of Virginia Refuge or other areas of the State.

Weekly tours that are conducted on Saturdays during the fall and winter would be moved to Sundays in order to eliminate the safety issues that this would cause.

Public Review and Comments: As part of the Comprehensive Conservation Planning (CCP) process for Eastern Shore of Virginia and Fisherman Island Refuges this compatibility determination will undergo extensive public review, including a comment period of 45 days following the release of the Draft Comprehensive Conservation Plan/Environmental Assessment (Draft CCP/EA).

Determination (check below):

_____ **Use is Not Compatible**

__X__ **Use is Compatible With Following Stipulations**

Stipulations to insure compatibility: The hunt program would be conducted in accordance with State hunt regulations. It would be reviewed annually to ensure deer management goals are achieved and that the program is providing a safe, high quality hunting experience for participants. Hunt season dates and bag limits would be adjusted as needed to achieve reduction of the resident breeding population of white-tailed deer. We would work with the State to determine safe numbers of hunters. The components of an Environmental Assessment (EA) would be satisfied through this Draft CCP/EA. A hunt plan would be written and approved before hunting occurs. The plan would be reviewed each year the management hunt is to take place and would provide overall documentation of permitted hunting, including the relationship of hunting to other refuge objectives.

To mitigate impacts that might cause an increase in the predator population, hunters would be required to field dress deer off the refuge. An area on the Eastern Shore of Virginia Refuge would be designated for this purpose. The refuge's no littering policy would be strictly enforced to reduce food and litter that may attract predators. Additionally, only antlerless deer would be hunted at Fisherman Island Refuge. This stipulation would assist in meeting our objective of reducing the number of breeding deer on the refuge.

Hunting from tree stands would be required and access to these stands would be within specified areas. Hunters would provide their own stand, but it must be placed in a designated location. This would reduce the amount of trampling to sensitive barrier island vegetation. Additionally, it would increase the safety of hunters that are on the island. A hunter orientation would be required of all hunters wishing to hunt on Fisherman Island. The orientation would include information ranging from safe access on and off the island to designated hunt stand locations to methods of reducing impacts on fragile barrier island vegetation.

This archery hunt would be conducted on the same dates as the Eastern Shore of Virginia Refuge's shotgun hunt for white-tailed deer. The late November/December dates occur after most neotropical migrant birds have departed the area, thus ensuring disturbance is minimized. Additionally, research on neotropical migrants takes place periodically on Fisherman Island during the migration season. The later hunt date would eliminate possible conflicts and safety issues between the two user groups.

An additional Refuge Officer would not be hired for the hunt on Fisherman Island Refuge. Rather, law enforcement officers that are present for the hunt on Eastern Shore of Virginia Refuge would also oversee the hunt on Fisherman Island.

Justification: Hunting is identified in the National Wildlife Refuge System Improvement Act of 1997 as a priority public use. A deer hunt at Fisherman Island National Wildlife Refuge is not expected to adversely impact the targeted species because the reduction of white-tailed deer may reduce the damage to feeding and cover habitat for neotropical migrant species. The expected results of the hunt are improved habitat and a quality hunt experience for participants. Hunting on Fisherman Island National Wildlife Refuge would not interfere with nor detract from the fulfillment of the National Wildlife Refuge System mission or the purposes of the refuge.

Signature: Refuge   Manager: _____
                                        (Signature and Date)

Concurrence: Regional   Chief: _____
                                        (Signature and Date)

Mandatory 10- or 15-year Re-evaluation Date: _____

Map F-4

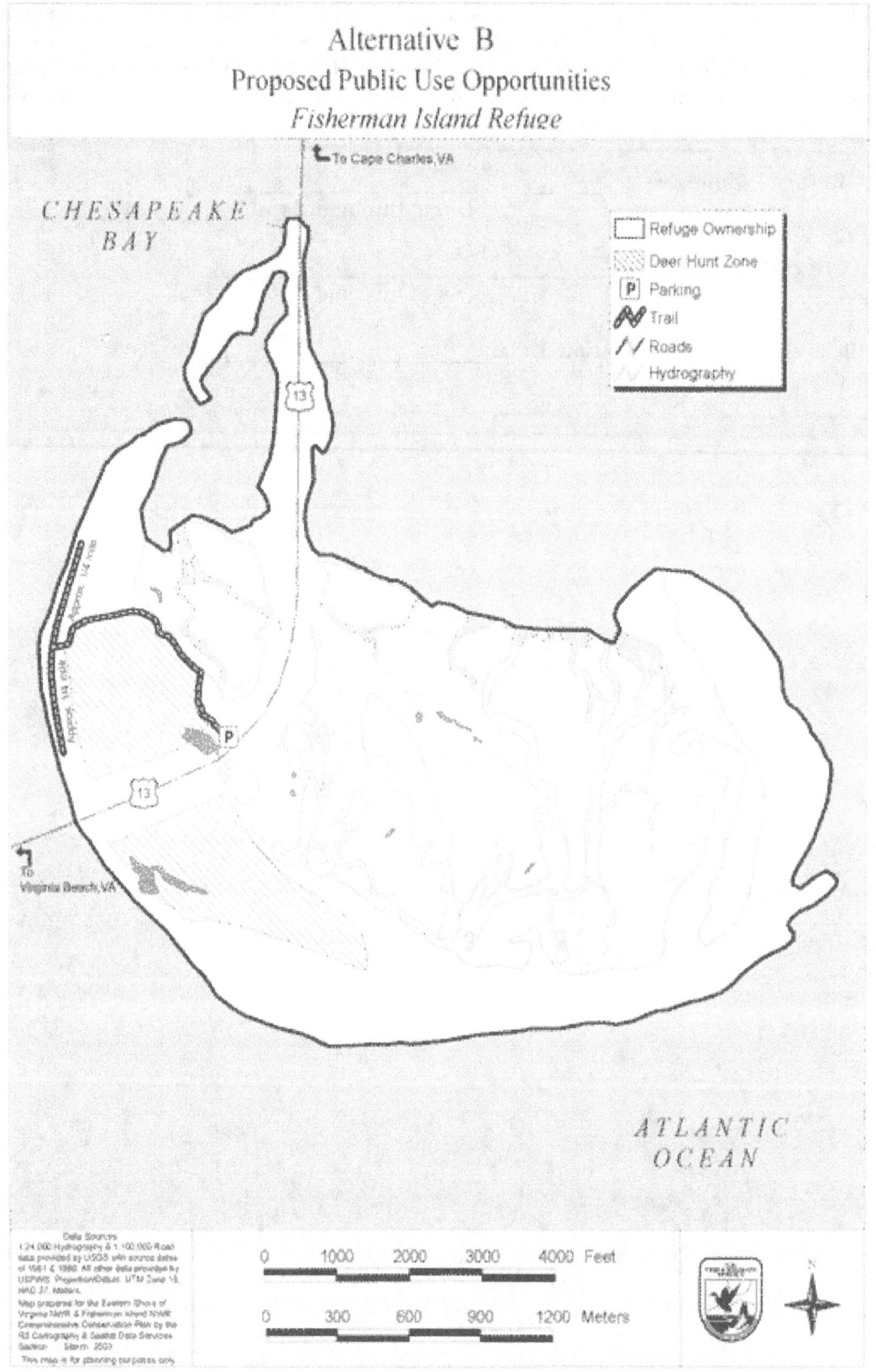

Alternative B
Proposed Public Use Opportunities
Fisherman Island Refuge

F-24

Description of Proposed Use: Wildlife Observation, Wildlife Photography, Interpretation and Environmental Education

Refuge Name: Fisherman Island National Wildlife Refuge

Establishing and Acquisition Authority(ies): Fisherman Island National Wildlife Refuge (Fisherman Island Refuge) was established under 16 U.S. Code 667b, Public Law 80-537, an Act authorizing the transfer of certain real property for wildlife, or other purposes. An additional parcel of land on the island was acquired under the Migratory Bird Conservation Act, 16 U.S.C. 715d.

Refuge Purpose(s):..... particular value in carrying out the national migratory bird management program. 16 U.S.C. 667b (An Act Authorizing the Transfer of Certain Real Property for Wildlife, or other purposes)

National Wildlife Refuge System Mission: To administer a national network of lands and waters for the conservation, management, and where appropriate, restoration of the fish, wildlife, and plant resources and their habitats within the United States for the benefit of present and future generations of Americans.

Description of Use:

A. What is the use? Is the use a priority use?
The uses are wildlife observation, wildlife photography, interpretation and environmental education. These uses are priority public uses, as identified in the National Wildlife Refuge Improvement Act (USFWS 1997).

B. Where would the use be conducted?
There is a 1.5 mile unimproved trail on Fisherman Island National Wildlife Refuge that goes from the parking area by the Chesapeake Bay Bridge Tunnel (Bridge-Tunnel) to the Chesapeake Bay. The staff at the Eastern Shore of Virginia National Wildlife Refuge (Eastern Shore of Virginia Refuge) conducts educational programs and guided interpretive walks on Fisherman Island Refuge from October 1 to March 15. Visitors learn about the U.S. Fish and Wildlife Service (Service) and the important role Fisherman Island Refuge plays in wildlife protection.

Wildlife Observation is the primary activity on the refuge. A small percentage of visitors who participate in wildlife observation are also interested in photographing wildlife.

C. When would the use be conducted?
All uses would be conducted within regular refuge hours, which are a half-hour before sunrise to a half-hour after sunset.

D. How would the use be conducted?
In Alternative B (the Proposed Action) we would continue with the above uses. There would be no additional opportunities for wildlife observation and photography, environmental education or interpretation on the refuge.

E. Why is the use being proposed?
Wildlife observation, wildlife photography, environmental education, and interpretation are priority public uses as defined by the National Wildlife Refuge System Administration Act of 1966, as amended by the National Wildlife Refuge System Improvement Act of 1997 (Public Law 105-57), and if compatible, are to receive enhanced consideration over other general public uses.

Availability of Resources: Because we are not expanding opportunities for wildlife observation and photography, environmental education or interpretation, no additional refuge resources would be required.

Anticipated Impacts of the Use: The four uses would provide visitors with a unique opportunity to observe wildlife and learn about the critical habitat we manage on the refuge.

Visitor use on Fisherman Island Refuge could potentially disturb colonial and beach nesting birds. Visitors could also trample sensitive beach vegetation and cause damage to beach dunes. Walking on the trail and beach tends to displace birds that are close to those areas.

Public Review and Comments: As part of the Comprehensive Conservation Plan (CCP) process for Eastern Shore of Virginia and Fisherman Island Refuges, this compatibility determination will undergo extensive public review, including a comment period of 45 days following the release of the Draft Comprehensive Conservation Plan/Environmental Assessment (Draft CCP/EA).

Determination (check below):

_____ **Use is Not Compatibility**

__X__ **Use is Compatible With Following Stipulations**

Stipulations Necessary to Ensure Compatibility: To limit disturbance to colonial and beach nesting birds during the migrating and breeding seasons, we would not allow visitors on Fisherman Island Refuge between March 30 and October 15. When visitors are allowed, they are escorted by a guide and are restricted to the road to prevent trampling of sensitive vegetation.

Closing the refuge to public use from March 15 to September 30 has an insignificant effect on the local economy. Most of the visitors who participate in guided tours of the refuge do not stay overnight at local hotels. Visitors may eat at local restaurants before or after visiting the refuge, so restaurants could gain more profit if tours of the refuge were held all year round.

Justification: One of the secondary goals of the National Wildlife Refuge System is to provide opportunities for the public to develop an understanding and appreciation for wildlife wherever those opportunities are compatible. Environmental education, interpretation, wildlife observation and photography are identified in the National Wildlife Refuge System Improvement Act of 1997 as priority public uses. These activities would not materially interfere with or detract from the fulfillment of the National Wildlife Refuge System mission or the purposes of the refuge.

Signature: **Refuge Manager:** _____
                                              (Signature and Date)

Concurrence: Regional Chief: _____
                                      (Signature and Date)

Mandatory 10- or 15-year Re-evaluation Date: _____

Description of Proposed Use: This interim compatibility determination covers priority, wildlife-dependent public uses (environmental education, interpretation, wildlife observation, photography, hunting and fishing) on lands proposed for acquisition.

Refuge Name: Eastern Shore of Virginia National Wildlife Refuge

Establishing and Acquisition Authority(ies): Eastern Shore of Virginia National Wildlife Refuge (Eastern Shore of Virginia Refuge) was established under 16 U.S. Code 667b, Public Law 80-537, an Act authorizing the transfer of certain real property for wildlife, or other purposes. Additional parcels of land were acquired under the Migratory Bird Conservation Act, 16 U.S.C. 715d.

Refuge Purpose(s): ..... particular value in carrying out the national migratory bird management program. 16 U.S.C. 667b (An Act Authorizing the Transfer of Certain Real Property for Wildlife, or other purposes)..... suitable for (1) incidental fish and wildlife-oriented recreational development, (2) the protection of natural resources, (3) the conservation of endangered species or threatened species ..... 16 U.S.C. 460k-1 (Refuge Recreation Act)..... for the development, advancement, management, conservation, and protection of fish and wildlife resources ..... 16 U.S.C. 742f(a)(4) ..... for the benefit of the United States Fish and Wildlife Service, in performing its activities and services. Such acceptance may be subject to the terms of any restrictive or affirmative covenant, or condition of servitude ..... 16 U.S.C. 742f(b)(1) (Fish and Wildlife Act of 1956)

National Wildlife Refuge System Mission: To administer a national network of lands and waters for the conservation, management, and where appropriate, restoration of the fish, wildlife, and plant resources and their habitats within the United States for the benefit of present and future generations of Americans.

Description of Use:

A. What is the use? Is the use a priority use?
The uses are environmental education, interpretation, wildlife observation, photography, hunting and fishing. These uses are priority public uses, as identified in the National Wildlife Refuge Improvement Act (USFWS 1997).

B. Where would the use be conducted?
The parcels identified in Alternative B (the Proposed Action) of the Draft Comprehensive Conservation Plan/Environmental Assessment (Draft CCP/EA), and in the proposed Land Protection Plan (include in the Draft CCP/EA as Appendix K) for Eastern Shore of Virginia Refuge, identify areas where the Service would seek to acquire land from willing sellers. Levels of current wildlife-dependent public use are not known for most of these areas. Since most of the parcels are in private ownership, we assume low to moderate levels of existing public use.

We have identified individual tracts of land for proposed acquisition; however, without conducting some baseline resource inventories of these lands, it is difficult to determine which lands would be best able to support wildlife-dependent recreational uses. In general, we would allow wildlife observation, photography, interpretation and education wherever these activities would least affect neotropical migratory bird populations. We estimate there would be at least one but no more than two trails each on the Chesapeake Bay side, the southern tip and the seaside areas of the proposed land acquisition area. If and when we acquire parcels adjacent to Kiptopeke State Park, we would work with the Park to establish a trail and other connections to give visitors a larger area on which to engage in wildlife-dependent recreational uses.

When we acquire parcels along the Chesapeake Bay, we would open those areas to shoreline fishing and possibly other wildlife-dependent public uses.

C. When would the use be conducted?
All uses would be conducted within regular refuge hours, which are a half-hour before sunrise to a half-hour after sunset. Hunting would be offered within legal hunting hours.

D. How would the use be conducted?
We would allow deer and small game hunting on lands to be acquired provided there would be minimal disturbance to neotropical migratory species. Deer and small game hunting would fall within the parameters of the State hunting seasons and would generally be permitted on forested tracts measuring 75 acres or more in size.

We would allow waterfowl hunting on any marsh blocks we acquire that are 200 acres or larger. Our waterfowl hunt season would fall within the parameters of the state waterfowl season.

Finally, we would partner with Northampton County and with local municipalities to help support local community fishing and hunting events.

E. Why is the use being proposed?
Hunting, fishing, wildlife observation, wildlife photography, environmental education, and interpretation are priority public uses as defined by the National Wildlife Refuge System Administration Act of 1966, as amended by the National Wildlife Refuge System Improvement Act of 1997 (Public Law 105-57), and if compatible, are to receive enhanced consideration over other general public uses.

Availability of Resources: No refuge resources would be devoted to interim public uses. Expenditures for the improvement of public use opportunities would be identified as projects in an updated Public Use Plan and in the Refuge Operating Needs System (RONS).

Before interim uses would be allowed under this compatibility determination, properties acquired would be posted. Posting would occur regardless of the potential for wildlife-dependent public uses at a site.

Anticipated Impacts on Service Lands, Waters or Interest: Within the proposed acquisition areas, current levels of use are not known for the six priority, wildlife-dependent uses defined in The National Wildlife Refuge System Improvement Act of 1997 (i.e., hunting, fishing, wildlife observation and photography, environmental education and interpretation). Impacts of such uses are expected to be minimal, provided the uses are only allowed in accordance with the stipulations listed below.

Some research suggests human intrusion in wildlife habitats, such as walking on trails, can cause disturbance to wildlife. One example is a study (Gutzwiller et. al, 1997) that showed human intrusion influences avian singing behavior in some species. During breeding season, the seasonal timing of male song affects the timing of territory establishments, male attraction, pair formation, egg laying, and transmission of information about breeding songs to young (Gutzwiller, et. al, 1997). Therefore, if human intrusion affects singing, it could ultimately affect reproduction and survival of some species. Another study (Riffell et. al, 1996) suggests that when repeated human intrusion recurs over an extended period of time, impacts on avian reproductive fitness have the potential to accumulate temporally at the individual, population and community levels. However, the refuge's main role in the life cycle of avian species is not during breeding but rather during migration.

Some wildlife disturbance and trampling of vegetation would occur from deer, small game and waterfowl hunting, as hunters walk around in designated areas. Shotgun noise from game and waterfowl hunting would cause some wildlife disturbance. Hunting can also cause conflict with other wildlife-dependent recreational uses such as wildlife observation and photography.

Opening land to public use can often result in litter, vandalism, and other illegal activities on Refuge lands.

Public Review and Comments: As part of the Comprehensive Conservation Plan (CCP) process for Eastern Shore of Virginia Refuge, this compatibility determination will undergo extensive public review, including a comment period of 45 days following the release of the Draft CCP/EA.

Determination (check below):

_____ **Use is Not Compatibility**

__X__ **Use is Compatible With Following Stipulations**

Stipulations to insure compatibility: Public use areas would be monitored at various times of the year to assess wildlife disturbance. We would include information about proper etiquette and the effects of human impacts on habitat and wildlife resources in refuge publications and flyers. Periodic law enforcement would ensure compliance with regulations and area closures, and would discourage vandalism.

To limit wildlife disturbance caused by human intrusion, we would limit access on some trails during the fall migration period to protect feeding and resting habitat for migratory birds. During this time, we would offer only guided tours or we may close trails for certain periods of time. All other times of the year, trails would be open to visitors during normal refuge hours.

We would only open shoreline areas of Chesapeake Bay properties to public use if we find there are no tiger beetles present there. If tiger beetles are found, we would survey the population, just as we propose to survey the population on the southern tip beach in Alternative B. Depending on what we learn about the population, we may allow seasonal use of the shoreline during the winter months, since tiger beetles are known to be able to withstand a moderate amount of public use.

To minimize disturbance to neotropical migratory species, we would permit small game hunting only after the major migration period, which is after December 1, and we would not allow pursuit dogs. All areas would be posted and monitored for disturbance.

We would minimize conflicts between game hunters and other users by hunting later in the season, when many of the prime photography and wildlife observation opportunities have past.

We would ensure resource protection and visitor safety on lands to be acquired by hiring full-time or seasonal law enforcement personnel to patrol areas and educate people about appropriate activities on refuge lands.

Justification: One of the secondary goals of the National Wildlife Refuge System is to provide opportunities for the public to develop an understanding and appreciation for wildlife wherever those opportunities are compatible. Hunting, fishing, environmental education, interpretation, wildlife observation and photography are identified in the National Wildlife Refuge System Improvement Act of 1997 as priority public uses. These activities can be accomplished without conflicting with the primary mission of Eastern Shore of Virginia Refuge. These activities would not materially interfere with or detract from the fulfillment of the National Wildlife Refuge System mission or the purposes of the refuge.

Signature: Refuge Manager: _____
                                            (Signature and Date)

Concurrence: Regional Chief: _____
                                      (Signature and Date)

Mandatory 10- or 15-year Re-evaluation Date: _____

References

Constanzo, Gary. June 2001. Personal Communication.

Gutzwiller, Kevin J. Elizabeth A. Kroese, Stanley H. Anderson, and Charles A. Wilkins. 1997. Does human intrusion alter the seasonal timing of avian song during breeding periods? The Auk. 114(1):55-65.

Riffell, Samuel K. Kevin J. Gutzwiller, and Stanley H. Anderson. 1996. Does repeated human intrusion cause cumulative declines in avian richness and abundance? Ecological Applications. 6(2). pp. 492-505.

U.S. Fish and Wildlife Service. May 1988. North American Waterfowl Management Plan: Atlantic Coast Joint Venture. 106 pp.

U.S. Fish and Wildlife Service. 1997 National Wildlife Refuge Improvement Act 1997. Public Law 105-57-Oct. 9, 1997.

Use: Research conducted by non-Service personnel

Refuge Name: Eastern Shore of Virginia National Wildlife Refuge

Establishing and Acquisition Authorities:
The Eastern Shore of Virginia National Wildlife Refuge, located in Northampton County, Virginia, was established in August 1984, by an Act Authorizing the Transfer of Certain Real Property for Wildlife, or other purposes (16 U.S.C. 667b-667d), as amended, and Lands acquired under the Refuge Recreation Act (16 U.S.C. 460k-460k-4) as amended, for one or more of the following purposes: " ...(1) incidental fish and wildlife -oriented recreational development, (2) the protection of natural resources, (3) the conservation of endangered species or threatened species ..."16 U.S.C. 460k-1.

Refuge Purpose(s):
 "... particular value in carrying out the national migratory bird management program." 16 U.S.C. 667b (An Act Authorizing the Transfer of Certain Real Property for Wildlife, or other purposes)

"... suitable for- (1) incidental fish and wildlife-oriented recreational development, (2) the protection of natural resources, (3) the conservation of endangered species or threatened species..." 16 U.S.C. 460k-1 (Refuge Recreation Act)

National Wildlife Refuge System Mission:
The mission of the National Wildlife Refuge System is "to administer a national network of lands and waters for the conservation, management, and where appropriate, restoration of the fish, wildlife, and plant resources and their habitats within the United States for the benefit of present and future generations of Americans."

Description of Use:
(a) What is the use? Is the use a priority public use?
The use is research conducted by non-Service personnel. Research conducted by non-Service personnel is not a priority public use of the Refuge System.

(b) Where would the use be conducted?
The location of the research will vary depending on the individual research project that is being conducted. The entire refuge is open and available for scientific research. An individual research project is usually limited to a particular habitat type, plant or wildlife species. On occasion research projects will encompass an assemblage of habitat types, plants or wildlife. The research location will be limited to those areas of the refuge that are absolutely necessary to conduct of the research project.

(c) When would the use be conducted?
The timing of the research will depend entirely on the individual research project that is being conducted. Scientific research will be allowed to occur on the refuge throughout the year. An individual research project could be short term in design, requiring one or two visits over the course of a few days. Other research projects could be multiple year studies that require daily visits to the study site. The timing of each individual research project will be limited to the minimum required to complete the project. If a research project occurs during the refuge hunting season, special precautions will be required and enforced to ensure public health and safety.

(d) How would the use be conducted?
The mechanics of the research will depend on the individual research project that is conducted. The methods of each research project will be scrutinized before it will be allowed to occur. No research project will be allowed to occur if it does not have an approved scientific method or if it compromises public health and safety.

(e) Why is this use being proposed?

Research by non-Service personnel is conducted by colleges, universities, Federal, State, and local agencies, non-governmental organizations, and qualified members of the general public to further the understanding of the natural environment and to improve the management of the refuge's natural resources. Much of the information generated by the research is applicable to management on and near the refuge. Most research projects on the Eastern Shore of Virginia study avian migration patterns. For example, researchers from the Center for Conservation Biology (CCB), affiliated with the College of William and Mary, have been mist netting saw-whet owls during fall migration for almost 10 years in order to study migration ecology and winter distribution of these birds. Another researcher from CCB has been banding raptors during fall migration for more than 20 years. This project has been looking at the concentration of flight paths of migrating raptors at the tip of the Delmarva Peninsula. The peregrine falcon is one of the project's focus species.

Researchers from the Coastal Virginia Wildlife Observatory (CVWO), a private non-profit research institute, conducted a spring banding project of neotropical migrants from 1999 through 2002. The main purpose was to determine migration ecology of this suite of birds. CVWO has also conducted butterfly and skipper surveys since 1995. Beginning in 1998, researchers also began tagging migrating monarch butterflies to learn about the migration ecology of these insects.

The Service will encourage and support research and management studies on refuge lands that will improve and strengthen natural resource management decisions. The refuge manager will encourage and seek research relative to approved refuge objectives that clearly improves land management and promotes adaptive management. Priority research addresses information that will better manage the Nation's biological resources and are generally considered important to: Agencies of the Department of Interior; the U.S. Fish and Wildlife Service; the National Wildlife Refuge System; and State Fish and Game Agencies, and that address important management issues or demonstrate techniques for management of species and/or habitats.

The refuge will also consider research for other purposes which may not be directly related to refuge-specific objectives, but contribute to the broader enhancement, protection, use, preservation and management of native populations of fish, wildlife and plants, and their natural diversity within the region or flyway. These proposals must comply with the Service's compatibility policy.

The refuge will maintain a list of research needs that will be provided to prospective researchers or organizations upon request. Refuge support of research directly related to refuge objectives may take the form of funding, in-kind services such as housing or use of other facilities, direct staff assistance with the project in the form of data collection, provision of historical records, conducting of management treatments, or other assistance as appropriate.

Availability of Resources:

The bulk of the cost for research is incurred in staff time to review research proposals, coordinate with researchers and write Special Use Permits. In some cases, a research project may only require one day of staff time to write a Special Use Permit. In other cases, a research project may take an accumulation of weeks, as the Refuge biologist must coordinate with students and advisors and accompany researchers on site visits. The Refuge biologist spends an average of seven weeks a year working full time on research projects conducted by outside researchers on both Fisherman Island and Eastern Shore of Virginia Refuges. At an hourly wage of approximately $25 (for a GS 11), this adds up to about $7,000 annually for resources spent on outside research for both refuges combined.

Anticipated Impacts of the Use:

The Service encourages approved research to further the understanding of the natural resources. Research by other than Service personnel adds greatly to the information base for Refuge Managers to make proper decisions. Disturbance to wildlife and vegetation by researchers could occur through observation, mist-netting, banding, and accessing the study area by foot or vehicle. It is possible that direct mortality could result as a by-product of research activities. Mist-netting saw-whet owls, for example, can cause stress, especially when birds are captured, banded and weighed. There have been occasional mortalities to these birds, namely when predators such as raccoons and cats reach the netted birds before researchers do.

Occasionally, a raptor has been injured during capture and/or banding.

Overall, however, allowing research to be conducted by non-Service personnel would have very little impact on Service interests. If the research project is conducted with professionalism and integrity, potential adverse impacts far outweigh the knowledge gained about an entire species.

Public Review and Comment:
As part of the CCP process for Eastern Shore of Virginia and Fisherman Island NWRs this compatibility determination will undergo extensive public review, including a comment period of 45 days following the release of the Draft CCP/EA.

Determination (check one below):

___ Use is Not Compatible

___ Use is Compatible With Following Stipulations

Stipulations Necessary to Ensure Compatibility:
All researchers will be required to submit a detailed research proposal following Service Policy (FWS Refuge Manual Chapter 4 Section 6). The refuge must be given at least 45 days to review proposals before initiation of research. If collection of wildlife is involved, the refuge must be given 60 days to review the proposal. Proposals will be prioritized and approved based on need, benefit, compatibility, and funding required.

Special Use Permits (SUP) will be issued for all research conducted by non-Service personnel. The SUP will list all conditions that are necessary to ensure compatibility. The Special Use Permits will also identify a schedule for annual progress reports and the submittal of a final report or scientific paper.

The Regional refuge biologists, other Service Divisions, and State agencies will be asked to review and comment on complex proposals.

All researchers will be required to obtain appropriate State and Federal permits.

Researchers would be required to take certain precautions aimed at avoiding incidental take or injury of an animal. For example, if an owl caught in a mist net is taken by a predator, the net would be closed down until the predator is found, trapped and removed. If a raptor injury occurs during banding, the bird would be taken to a vet and the operation would be shut down.

Justification: The Service encourages approved research to further understanding of refuge natural resources. Research by non- Service personnel adds greatly to the information base for Refuge Managers to make proper decisions. Research conducted by non-Service personnel will not materially interfere with or detract from the mission of the National Wildlife Refuge System or the purposes for which the Refuge was established.

Signature - Refuge Manager: _____
(Signature and Date)

Concurrence - Regional Chief: _____
(Signature and Date)

Mandatory 10- or 15-year Reevaluation Date: _____

Literature Cited:

Department of the Interior. <u>Departmental Manual</u>. Washington, D.C.: U.S. Government Printing Office

U.S. Fish and Wildlife Service. 1985. <u>Refuge Manual</u>. Washington, D.C.: U.S. Government Printing Office.

Use: Research conducted by non-Service personnel

Refuge Name: Fisherman Island National Wildlife Refuge

Establishing and Acquisition Authority: Fisherman Island National Wildlife Refuge was established under 16 U.S. Code 667b, Public Law 80-537, an Act authorizing the transfer of certain real property for wildlife, or other purposes. An additional parcel of land on the island was acquired under the Migratory Bird Conservation Act, 16 U.S.C. 715d.

Refuge Purpose(s): ..... particular value in carrying out the national migratory bird management program. 16 U.S.C. 667b (An Act Authorizing the Transfer of Certain Real Property for Wildlife, or other purposes).

National Wildlife Refuge System Mission:
The mission of the National Wildlife Refuge System is "to administer a national network of lands and waters for the conservation, management, and where appropriate, restoration of the fish, wildlife, and plant resources and their habitats within the United States for the benefit of present and future genera- tions of Americans."

Description of Use:

(a) What is the use? Is the use a priority public use?
The use is research conducted by non-Service personnel. Research conducted by non-Service personnel is not a priority public use of the Refuge System.

(b) Where would the use be conducted?
The location of the research will vary depending on the individual research project that is being con- ducted. The entire refuge is open and available for scientific research. An individual research project is usually limited to a particular habitat type, plant or wildlife species. On occasion research projects will encompass an assemblage of habitat types, plants or wildlife. The research location will be limited to those areas that are absolutely necessary to conduct of the research project.

(c) When would the use be conducted?
The timing of the research will depend entirely on the individual research project that is being con- ducted. Scientific research will be allowed to occur throughout the year. An individual research project could be short term in design, requiring one or two visits over the course of a few days. Other research projects could be multiple year studies that require daily visits to the study site. The timing of each research project will be limited to the minimum required to complete the project. If the refuge is opened to hunting in the future, special precautions will be required and enforced to ensure public health and safety during the hunt season.

(d) How would the use be conducted?
The mechanics of the research will depend on the individual research project that is conducted. The methods of each research project will be scrutinized well before it will be allowed to occur. No research project will be allowed to occur if it does not have an approved scientific method or if it compromises public health and safety.

(e) Why is this use being proposed?
Research by non-Service personnel is conducted by colleges, universities, Federal, State, and local agencies, non-governmental organizations, and qualified members of the general public to further the understanding of the natural environment and to improve the management of the refuge's natural re- sources. Much of the information generated by the research is applicable to management on and near

the refuge. Most research projects on Fisherman Island study shoreline dynamics and geology, migrating birds and colonial nesting waterbirds. For example, research on shoreline and landscape dynamics of Fisherman Island has been used to determine the origin and development of the island. A student from the College of William and Mary has been monitoring the productivity of American oystercatchers. Beginning in 2003, the student will band American oystercatcher chicks to determine wintering migration distribution.

A group of volunteer researchers has conducted colonial waterbird surveys in mid-June on all the Virginia barrier islands, including Fisherman Island, for 29 years, to discover trends associated with these birds. Another researcher has been studying water resources and vegetation patterns on Fisherman Island.

The Service will encourage and support research and management studies on refuge lands that will improve and strengthen natural resource management decisions. The refuge manager will encourage and seek research relative to approved refuge objectives that clearly improves land management and promotes adaptive management. Priority research addresses information that will better manage the Nation's biological resources and are generally considered important to: Agencies of the Department of Interior; the U.S. Fish and Wildlife Service; the National Wildlife Refuge System; and State Fish and Game Agencies, and that address important management issues or demonstrate techniques for management of species and/or habitats.

The refuge will also consider research for other purposes which may not be directly related to refuge-specific objectives, but contributes to the broader enhancement, protection, use, preservation and management of native populations of fish, wildlife and plants, and their natural diversity within the region or flyway. These proposals must comply with the Service's compatibility policy.

The refuge will maintain a list of research needs that will be provided to prospective researchers or organizations upon request. Refuge support of research directly related to refuge objectives may take the form of funding, in-kind services such as housing or use of other facilities, direct staff assistance with the project in the form of data collection, provision of historical records, conducting of management treatments, or other assistance as appropriate.

Availability of Resources:
The bulk of the cost for research is incurred in staff time to review research proposals, coordinate with researchers and write Special Use Permits. In some cases, a research project may only require one day of staff time to write a Special Use Permit. In other cases, a research project may take an accumulation of weeks, as the Refuge biologist must coordinate with students and advisors and accompany researchers on site visits. The Refuge biologist spends an average of seven weeks a year working full time on research projects conducted by outside researchers on both Fisherman Island and Eastern Shore of Virginia Refuges. At an hourly wage of approximately $25 (for a GS 11), this adds up to about $7,000 annually for resources spent on outside research for both refuges combined.

Anticipated Impacts of the Use:
The Service encourages approved research to further the understanding of the natural resources. Research by other than Service personnel adds greatly to the information base for Refuge Managers to make proper decisions. Disturbance to wildlife and vegetation by researchers could occur through observation, banding, and accessing the study area by foot or vehicle. It is possible that direct mortality could result as a by-product of research activities. For example, royal tern chick mortalities have occurred when chicks piled on top of each other and suffered from heat exhaustion. Mortalities have also occurred when gulls preyed on chicks returning to their nest after being banded.

There have been no known mortalities in the American oystercatcher colony due to researcher presence. However, these birds are easily spooked and will readily fly off their nest when a researcher approaches, even from a long distance. Nest abandonment can leave eggs or chicks vulnerable to heat or predators.

Overall, however, allowing research to be conducted by non-Service personnel would have little impact on Service interests. If the research project is conducted with professionalism and integrity, potential adverse impacts far outweigh the knowledge gained about an entire species.

Public Review and Comment:
As part of the CCP process for Eastern Shore of Virginia and Fisherman Island NWRs this compatibility determination will undergo extensive public review, including a comment period of 45 days following the release of the Draft CCP/EA.

Determination (check one below):

___ Use is Not Compatible

___ Use is Compatible With Following Stipulations

Stipulations Necessary to Ensure Compatibility:
All researchers will be required to submit a detailed research proposal following Service Policy (FWS Refuge Manual Chapter 4 Section 6). The refuge must be given at least 45 days to review proposals before initiation of research. If collection of wildlife is involved, the refuge must be given 60 days to review the proposal. Proposals will be prioritized and approved based on need, benefit, compatibility, and funding required.

Special Use Permits (SUP) will be issued for all research conducted by non-Service personnel. The SUP will list all conditions that are necessary to ensure compatibility. The Special Use Permits will also identify a schedule for annual progress reports and the submittal of a final report or scientific paper.

The Regional refuge biologists, other Service Divisions, and State agencies may be asked to review and comment on certain proposals.

All researchers will be required to obtain appropriate State and Federal permits.

Research that involves banding birds would be conducted early in the day to avoid heat stress on chicks or on eggs that may be left exposed when adults fly off the nest. Researchers would minimize the number of times they visit a bird colony so as to minimize nest abandonment. In the case where a large number of birds are banded at once, the researcher would be asked to recruit a large group of helpers to ensure the banding goes quickly.

Justification: The Service encourages approved research to further understanding of refuge natural resources. Research by non- Service personnel adds greatly to the information base for Refuge Managers to make proper decisions. Research conducted by non-Service personnel will not materially interfere with or detract from the mission of the National Wildlife Refuge System or the purposes for which the Refuge was established.

Signature - Refuge Manager: _____
                                    (Signature and Date)

Concurrence - Regional Chief: _____
                                    (Signature and Date)

Mandatory 10- or 15-year Reevaluation Date: _____

Literature Cited:

Department of the Interior. <u>Departmental Manual</u>. Washington, D.C.: U.S. Government Printing Office

U.S. Fish and Wildlife Service. 1985. <u>Refuge Manual</u>. Washington, D.C.: U.S. Government Printing Office.

Appendix G

Appendix G:

Refuge Operations Needs System (RONS) and Maintenance Management System (MMS) Project Lists

Terms used in this appendix:

Project: This list includes proposed projects expected to cost more than $15,000. Table G-1 includes those projects currently in the RONS database. Tables G-1 and G-2 include those projects proposed in the CCP Alternatives.

Project Number: This is the number used to identify the project in our Regional database system.

Tier: Tier 1 projects are given priority over Tier 2 projects.

Regional Ranking: This number indicates the project's rank in relation to all other similar refuge projects in Region 5.

Refuge Rank: This number indicates the project's rank in relation to all other projects on the Refuge. The number "999" indicates the Refuge has not ranked the project.

FTE: Full Time Staffing Equivalent. One FTE equals one person working full time for one whole year; seasonal employees are considered 0.5 FTE.

First Year Cost: Estimated costs incurred during the first year of a project - typically higher than recurring costs, due to construction, equipment purchased, or other start-up expenses.

Recurring Cost: Estimated average annual project cost for subsequent years; includes recurring salary and maintenance costs.

Project duration: Estimate length of time for each project. Since the CCP will be revised every 15 years, the "maximum project duration" is 15 years, even though some projects may continue into the next planning cycle.

ESV NWR and FSH NWR: These are the abbreviations for Eastern Shore of Virginia (ESV) National Wildlife Refuge (NWR) and Fisherman Island (FSH) NWR. These abbreviations are used throughout the matrices to clarify which projects correspond to which refuge.

Table G-1: Proposed projects currently in the RONs database (FY2003).

Project #	Project Description	Tier	Refuge Rank	Regional Rank	FTEs	First Year Cost ($1,000)	Recurring Cost ($1,000)	Project Duration (yrs.)
00006	Protect visitor safety and refuge resources	1	1	175	1	$117	$52	15
99004	Establish a biological program	2	1	10	1	$95	$74	15
00003	Control non-native plant species	1	3	199	0	$36	$12	15
02002	Office space for law enforcement and other mission critical staff	2	5	60	0	$45	0	1
02001	Wise Point interpretive kiosk	2	6	61	0	$50	0	1
99002	Initiate inventorying and monitoring of biological resources	1	7	50	0	$174	$34	15
02004	Wise Point sediment and water quality testing	2	9	65	0	$30	$5	15
00017	Improve maintenance of refuge infrastructure and equipment (Main/Equip Op)	1	10	30	1	$122	$57	15
00015	Inventory resources and apply adaptive management techniques (bio/biotech)	1	11	17	1	$128	$63	15
00016	Protect resources and ensure public safety (law enforcement officer)	1	12	12	1	$129	$64	15
02003	Eradicate exotic phragmites	2	13	66	0	$27	$2	15
00008	Construct 2 vehicle pull-offs with interpretive panels	2	14	30	0	$32	0	1
93107	Enhance environmental education programs	2	15	30	0	$102	$6	15
00012	Construct a public boat ramp	2	15	999	2	$633	$88	15
99009	Design a Geographical Information System (GIS) database	2	16	359	0	$29	$5	15

Table G-1 (continued): Proposed projects currently in the RONs database (FY2003).

Project #	Project Description	Tier	Refuge Rank	Regional Rank	FTEs	First Year Cost ($1,000)	Recurring Cost ($1,000)	Project Duration (yrs.)
00013	Refuge publications	2	17	600	0	$23	$6	15
01003	Facilitate acquisition and easement efforts to protect migratory bird habitat on the lower Delmarva Peninsula	2	18	999	1	$114	$65	15
01008	Monitor invasive species response to various control methods	2	19	999	1	$38	$36	15
01006	Construct boardwalk and overlook for new Wise Point trail	2	20	999	0	$32	$2	15
01001	Develop interpretive display and environmental education workshops	2	21	999	0	$30	$0	1
01009	Treat 125 acres of invasive plants	2	22	999	0	$29	$14	15
93111	Expand environmental education and interpretive programs	2	23	999	0	$65	0	2
01010	Regional Barrier Beach Management Network (RBBMN)	2	24	999	1	$65	$40	15
01007	Determine forest management techniques for Habitat Management	2	25	999	0	$26	$5	15
00002	Grassland habitat restoration	2	26	414	0	$44	$4	8
00005	Restore shrub and mixed hardwood habitat for migratory birds	2	27	385	0	$65	$2	5
01005	Analyze the socioeconomic benefits of the refuges to Northampton County	2	28	999	0	$50	0	5
01004	Construct demonstration gardens emphasizing native plant conservation for migratory birds	2	29	999	0	$22	$5	15
01002	Coordinate the creation, development, and mentoring of a refuge "Friends" group	2	30	999	0.5	$46	$19	15
00009	Three-mile bike trail along old railroad right-of-way	2	33	30	0	$44	$6	2

Tables G-2 and G-3 do not include a project number, Tier, Refuge rank or Regional Rank because they are proposed RONS projects. They are not in the current RONS system, and therefore have not been assigned a project number and have not been ranked.

Table G-2: Additional biological projects proposed for Alternative B, none of which are currently identified in the RONS database.

Project Description	FTEs	First Year Cost ($1,000)	Recurring Cost ($1,000)	Project Duration
Hire a seasonal biological technician to assist in bird, mammal, reptile, and amphibian surveys on ESV and FSH NWRs, and to assist in tiger beetle surveys on ESV NWR's southern tip beach	.5 seasonal biotechnician	$15	$15	15
Contract a sensitive plant/florists survey on FSH NWR; contract an invertebrate survey and a tiger beetle larval survey for both refuges	0	$36	$1 (for 3-year beetle study)	3
Expand public tours on FSH NWR	.5	$55	$22	15
Study predation on colonial nesting birds on FSH NWR	0	$57	$16	3

Table G-3: Additional public use project proposed for Alternative B which is not currently identified in the RONS database.

Project Description	FTEs	First Year Cost ($1,000)	Recurring Cost ($1,000)	Project Duration
Hire a Recreational Assistant to help develop 9 interpretive displays for trail kiosks, develop table top exhibits for outreach, update 3 interpretive signs; develop 11 new environmental lesson plans, annual teacher's workshops, photography workshops, and a series of monthly educational programs	1.0 (GS-5 Recreational Assistant)	$50	$34	15

Grand Totals	Alternative A	Alternative B
year 1 project costs	$2,442,000 (assuming all RONS projects are funded)	$213,000 increase from Alternative A
recurring project costs	$666,000	$88,000 increase from Alternative A

Table G-4. Refuge Maintenance Management System.

Project #	Project Name	Refuge Rank	Regional Rank	Cost Estimate ($1,000)
02001	CN Wise Point Road and parking	1	999	$300
02003	Replace unsafe Wise Point docks, ramp, bulkhead	2	125	$445
02004	Replace two refuge residences	2	261	$470
02005	Clean up and construct new firearms shooting range	3	888	$10,000
97001	Repair leaking Visitor Center roof and seal coat parking lots	3	70	$64
97003	Replace maintenance building heating system	4	72	$25
98507	Replace deteriorated displays/exhibits	5	193	$125
01006	Replace 1989 Chevy pickup	6	138	$19
93016	Phase 1: Resurface public use road (1.54 miles) and parking	7	53	$500
00008	Replace radio system to convert to 2005 standards	8	73	$82
99004	Replace leaky windows and siding in four refuge quarters	9	999	$43
00007	Replace worn-out Lowboy Trailer	10	215	$10
93035	Replace 1975 farm tractor	11	50	$50
01005	Replace 1994 Ford Taurus station wagon	12	219	$19
01003	Remove tower on FSH NWR	13	999	$10
01002	Remove water plant well houses on ESV NWR	14	999	$36
01001	Remove GATR tract communications building and tower	15	999	$68
01004	Remove GATR generator and pump house	16	999	$31
00003	Rehabilitate trail and fishing facilities and office	17	565	$42
93016	Phase II: Rehabilitate paved road (1.34 miles)	18	500	$500
00004	Rehabilitate Visitor Center parking lot with seal coat	99	999	$8
93107	Enhance environmental education	999	51	$102
00008 (R)	Construct two vehicle pull-outs with interpretive panels	999	52	$32
00009	Bike trail connection from Refuge to State Park	999	53	$44

Appendix H

Appendix H:

Glossary of Terms

Glossary of Terms

access – the state or quality of being easy to approach or enter.

accretion – slow addition to land by deposition of water-borne sediment.

agricultural land – nonforested land, due to its current or recent use for orchards, pasture, hay or crops.

alternative – a reasonable way to fix the identified problem or satisfy the stated need (40 CFR 1500.2) [see also management alternative below].

aquatic – growing in, living in, or dependent upon water.

biological or natural diversity – the variety of life in all its forms.

breeding habitat – habitat used by migratory birds or other animals during the breeding season.

buffer zones – protective land borders around critical habitats or water bodies that reduce runoff and nonpoint source pollution loading; areas created or sustained to lessen the negative effects of land development on animals and plants and their habitats.

CFR – Code of Federal Regulations.

community - the area or locality in which a group of people resides and shares the same government.

community type – a particular assemblage of plants and animals, named for the characteristic plants.

compatible use – an allowed use that will not materially interfere with or detract from the purposes for which the unit was established (Service Manual 602 FW 1.4).

compatibility determination – a compatibility determination is required for a wildlife-dependant recreational use or any other public use of a refuge. A compatible use is one which, in the sound professional judgement of the Refuge Manager, will not materially interfere with or detract from fulfillment of the Refuge System Mission or refuge purpose(s)

concern – see Issue.

conservation – the management of natural resources to prevent loss or waste. Management actions may include preservation, restoration, and enhancement.

cool-season grass – introduced grass for crop and pastureland that grows in spring and fall and is dormant during hot summer months.

cooperative agreement – the legal instrument used when the principal purpose of the transaction is the transfer of money, property, services or anything of value to a recipient in order to accomplish a public purpose authorized by Federal statute and substantial involvement between the Service and the recipient is anticipated.

cultural resource inventory – a professionally conducted study designed to locate and evaluate evidence of cultural resources present within a defined geographic area. Inventories may involve various levels, including background literature search, comprehensive field examination to identify all exposed physical manifestations of cultural resources, or sample inventory to project site distribution and density over a larger area. Evaluation of identified cultural resources to determine eligibility for the National Register follows the criteria found in 36 CFR 60.4 (Service Manual 614 FW 1.7).

cultural resource overview – a comprehensive document prepared for a field office that discusses, among other things, its prehistory and cultural history, the nature and extent of known cultural resources, previous research, management objectives, resource management conflicts or issues, and a general statement on how program objectives should be met and conflicts resolved. An overview should reference or incorporate information form a field offices background or literature search described in Section VIII. of the Cultural Resource Management Handbook (Service Manual 614 FW 1.7).

database – a collection of data arranged for ease and speed of analysis and retrieval, usually computerized.

designated wilderness area – an area designated by the United States Congress to be managed as part of the National Wilderness Preservation System (Draft Service Manual 610 FW 1.5).

digitizing – the process of converting information from paper maps into geographically referenced electronic files for a geographic information system (GIS).

easement – an agreement by which a landowner gives up or sells one of the rights on his/her property. For example, a landowner may donate a right of way across his/her property to allow community members access to a river. See also conservation easement.

ecosystem – a natural community of organisms interacting with its physical environment, regarded as a unit.

ecotourism – a type of tourism that maintains and preserves natural resources as a basis for promoting economic growth and development resulting from visitation to an area.

ecosystem approach – a way of looking at socio-economic and environmental information based on the boundaries of ecosystems rather than based on town, city, and county boundaries.

emergent wetland – wetlands dominated by erect, rooted, herbaceous plants.

endangered species – a federally protected species which is in danger of extinction throughout all or a significant portion of its range.

environmental education – education aimed at producing a citizenry that is knowledgeable concerning the biophysical environment and its associated problems, aware of how to help solve these problems, and motivated to work toward their solution.

Environmental Assessment (EA) – A concise public document, prepared in compliance with the National Environmental Policy Act, that briefly discusses the purpose and need for an action, alternatives to such action, and provides sufficient evidence and analysis of impacts to determine whether to prepare an environmental impact statement or finding of no significant impact (40 CFR 1508.9).

Environmental Impact Statement (EIS) – A detailed written statement required by section 102(2)(C) of the National Environmental Policy Act, analyzing the environmental impacts of a proposed action, adverse effects of the project that cannot be avoided, alternative courses of action, short-tern uses of the environment versus the maintenance and enhancement of long-term productivity, and any irreversible and irretrievable commitment of resources (40 CFR 1508.11).

exemplary community type – an outstanding example of a particular community type.

extirpated – no longer occurring in a given geographic area.

federal land – public land owned by the Federal government, including lands such as National Forests, National Parks and National Wildlife Refuges.

Federal-listed species – a species listed under the federal Endangered Species Act of 1973, as amended, either as endangered, threatened or species at risk (formerly candidate species).

Finding of No Significant Impact (FONSI) – A document prepared in compliance with the National Environmental Policy Act, supported by an environmental assessment, that briefly presents why a Federal action will have no significant effect on the human environment and for which an environmental impact statement, therefore, will not be prepared (40 CFR 1508.13).

forbs – A flowering plant, excluding grasses, sedges, and rushes, that does not have a woody stem and dies back to the ground at the end of the growing season.

forested land – land dominated by trees. For the purposes of the impacts analysis in this document, all forested land was assumed to have the potential to be occasionally harvested, and forested land owned by timber companies was assumed to be harvested on a more intensive, regular schedule.

forested wetlands – wetlands dominated by trees.

geographic information system (GIS) – a computerized system used to compile, store, analyze and display geographically referenced information. Can be used to overlay information layers containing the distributions of a variety of biological and physical features.

habitat fragmentation – breaking up of a specific habitat into smaller unconnected areas. A habitat area that is too small may not provide enough space to maintain a breeding population of the species in question.

habitat conservation – the protection of an animal or plant's habitat to ensure that the use of that habitat by the animal or plant is not altered or reduced.

habitat – the place where a particular type of plant or animal lives. An organism's habitat must provide all of the basic requirements for life and should be free of harmful contaminants.

interjurisdictional fish – populations of fish that are managed by two or more states or national or tribal governments because of the scope of their geographic distributions or migrations.

interpretive facilities – structures that provides information about an event, place or thing by a variety of means including printed materials, audiovisuals or multimedia materials. Examples of these would be kiosks which offer printed materials and audiovisuals, signs and trailheads.

interpretive materials – any tool used to provide or clarify information, explain events or things, or serve to increase awareness and understanding of the events or things. Examples of these would be: (1) printed materials such as brochures, maps or curriculum materials; (2) audio/visual materials such as videotapes, films, slides, or audio tapes; and (3) interactive multimedia materials, such as cd–rom and other computer technology.

issue – any unsettled matter that requires a management decision; e.g., a Service initiative, an opportunity, a management problem, a threat to the resources of the unit, a conflict in uses, a public concerns, or the presence of an undesirable resource condition. Issues should be documented, described, and analyzed in the CMP even if resolution cannot be accomplished during the planning process (Service Manual 602 FW 1.4).

land trusts – organizations dedicated to conserving land by purchasing land, receiving donations of lands, or accepting conservation easements from landowners.

local land – public land owned by local governments, including community or county parks, or municipal watersheds.

local agencies – generally referring to municipal governments, regional planning commissions or conservation groups.

long term protection – mechanisms such as fee title acquisition, conservation easements or binding agreements with landowners that ensure land use and land management practices will remain compatible with maintenance of the species population at the site.

management alternative – a set of objectives and the strategies needed to accomplish each objective (Service Manual 602 FW 1.4).

management concern – see Issue.

management opportunity – see Issue.

management plan – a plan that guides future land management practices on a tract of land.

management strategy – a general approach to meet unit objectives. A strategy may be broad, or it may be detailed enough to guide implementation through specific actions, tasks, and projects (Service Manual 602 FW 1.4).

mission statement – succinct statement of the unit's purpose and reason for being.

mitigation – actions taken to compensate for the negative effects of a particular project. Wetland mitigation usually takes the form of restoration or enhancement of a previously damaged wetland or creation of a new wetland.

National Environmental Policy Act of 1969 (NEPA) – requires all agencies, including the Service, to examine the environmental impacts of their actions, incorporate environmental information, and use public participation in the planning and implementation of all actions. Federal agencies must integrate NEPA with other planning requirements, and prepare appropriate NEPA documents to facilitate better environmental decision making (from 40 CFR 1500).

National Wildlife Refuge System – all lands and waters and interests therein administered by the Service as wildlife refuges, wildlife ranges, wildlife management areas, waterfowl production areas, and other areas for the protection and conservation of fish and wildlife, including those that are threatened with extinction.

native plant – a plant that has grown in the region since the last glaciation and occurred before European settlement.

non-point source pollution – nutrients or toxic substances that enter water from dispersed and uncontrolled sites.

Notice of Intent (NOI) – a notice that an environmental impact statement will be prepared and considered (40 CFR 1508.22). Published in the Federal Register.

outdoor education projects – any cooperative ventures that combine the financial and staff resources to develop and implement outdoor education activities such as labs, field trips, surveys, or monitoring/sampling efforts.

outdoor education – educational activities that take place in an outdoor setting.

Partners for Wildlife Program – a voluntary habitat restoration program undertaken by the Fish and Wildlife Service in cooperation with other governmental agencies, public and private organizations, and private landowners to improve and protect fish and wildlife habitat on private lands while leaving the land in private ownership.

partnership – a contract or agreement entered into by two or more individuals, groups of individuals, organizations or agencies in which each agrees to furnish a part of the capital or some in–kind service, i.e., labor, for a mutually beneficial enterprise.

payment in lieu of taxes – see Revenue Sharing Act of 1935, Chapter One, Legal Context.

planning area – The area upon which the planning effort will focus. A planning area may include lands outside existing planning unit boundaries currently studied for inclusion in the Refuge System and/or partnership planning efforts. It may also include watersheds or ecosystems outside of our jurisdiction that affect the planning unit.

population monitoring – assessments of the characteristics of populations to ascertain their status and establish trends related to their abundance, condition, distribution, or other characteristics.

prescribed fire – the application of fire to wildland fuels to achieve identified land use objectives (Service Manual 621 FW 1.7), either from natural or intentional ignition.

private land – land that is owned by a private individual, group of individuals, or non– governmental organization.

private landowner – any individual, group of individuals or non–governmental organization that owns land.

private organization – any non–governmental organization.

protection – mechanisms such as fee title acquisition, conservation easements or binding agreements with landowners that ensure land use and land management practices will remain compatible with maintenance of the species population at the site.

public – individuals, organizations, and groups; officials of Federal, State, and local government agencies; Indian tribes; and foreign nations. It may include anyone outside the core planning team. It includes those who may or may not have indicated an interest in the Service issues and those who do or do not realize that Service decisions may affect them.

public involvement – a process that offers impacted and interested individuals and organizations an opportunity to become informed about, and to express their opinions on Service actions and policies. In the process, these views are studied thoroughly and thoughtful consideration of public views is given in shaping decisions for refuge management.

public involvement plan – broad long term guidance for involving the public in the comprehensive planning process.

public land – land that is owned by the local, state, or Federal government.

rare species – species identified in Appendix A as Species of Special Emphasis due to their uncommon occurrence within the planning area.

rare community types – plant community types classified as rare by any of the four state Natural Heritage Programs. The types are listed in Appendix A.

Record of Decision (ROD) – a concise public record of decision prepared by the Federal agency, pursuant to NEPA, that contains a statement of the decision, identification of all alternatives considered, identification of the environmentally preferable alternative, a statement as to whether all practical means to avoid or minimize environmental harm from the alternative selected have been adopted (and if not, why they were not), and a summary of monitoring and enforcement where applicable for any mitigation CFR 1505.2).

refuge goals – descriptive, open-ended and often broad statements of desired future conditions that convey a purpose but do not define measurable units.

refuge purposes – the purposes specified in or derived from the law, proclamation, executive order, agreement, public land order, donation document, or administrative memorandum establishing, authorizing, or expanding a refuge, a refuge unit, or refuge subunit, and any subsequent modification of the original establishing authority for additional conservation purposes (Service Manual 602 FW 1.4).

refuge lands – those lands in which the Service holds full interest in fee title, or partial interest such as easements.

restoration – the artificial manipulation of a habitat to restore it to its former condition. Involves taking a degraded grassland and re-establishing habitat for native plants and animals. Restoration usually involves the planting of native grasses and forbs, and may include shrub removal and prescribed burning.

species at risk – a species being considered for listing as a federally endangered or threatened species.

species of concern – a species not on the federal list of threatened or endangered species, but a species for which the Service or one of its partners has concerns.

state land – public land owned by a state such as state parks or state wildlife management areas.

state agencies – generally referring to natural resource arms of the state governments of Virginia.

step-down management plans – step-down management plans describe management strategies and implementation schedules. Step-down management plans are a series of plans dealing with specific management subjects (e.g., croplands, wilderness, and fire) (Service Manual 602 FW 1.4).

stopover habitat – habitat used during bird migration for rest and feeding.

threatened species – a federally protected species which is likely to become an endangered species within the foreseeable future throughout all or a significant portion of its range.

trust resource – one that through law or administrative act is held in trust for the people by the government. A federal trust resource is one for which trust responsibility is given in part to the federal government through federal legislation or administrative act. Generally, federal trust resources are those considered to be of national or international importance no matter where they occur, such as endangered species and species such as migratory birds and fish that regularly move across state lines. In addition to species, trust resources include cultural resources protected through federal historic preservation laws, nationally important and threatened habitats, notably wetlands, navigable waters, and public lands such as state parks and national wildlife refuges.

unfragmented habitat – large blocks of unbroken habitat of a particular type.

upland – dry ground; other than wetlands.

vision statement – concise statement of what the unit could be in the next 10 to 15 years.

warm-season grass – native prairie grass that puts on the most growth during summer when cool-season grasses are dormant.

wetlands – The U.S. Fish and Wildlife Service's definition of wetlands states that "Wetlands are lands transitional between terrestrial and aquatic systems where the water table is usually at or near the surface or the land is covered by shallow water." (Cowardin et al 1979)

wilderness – see designated wilderness.

wildlife management – the practice of manipulating wildlife populations, either directly through regulating the numbers, ages, and sex ratios harvested, or indirectly by providing favorable habitat conditions and alleviating limiting factors.

Appendix I

Appendix I:
Staffing Charts

U.S. Fish and Wildlife Service
Northeast Region
Regional Chief, National Wildlife Refuge System
Eastern Shore of Virginia National Wildlife Refuge
(Fisherman Island)

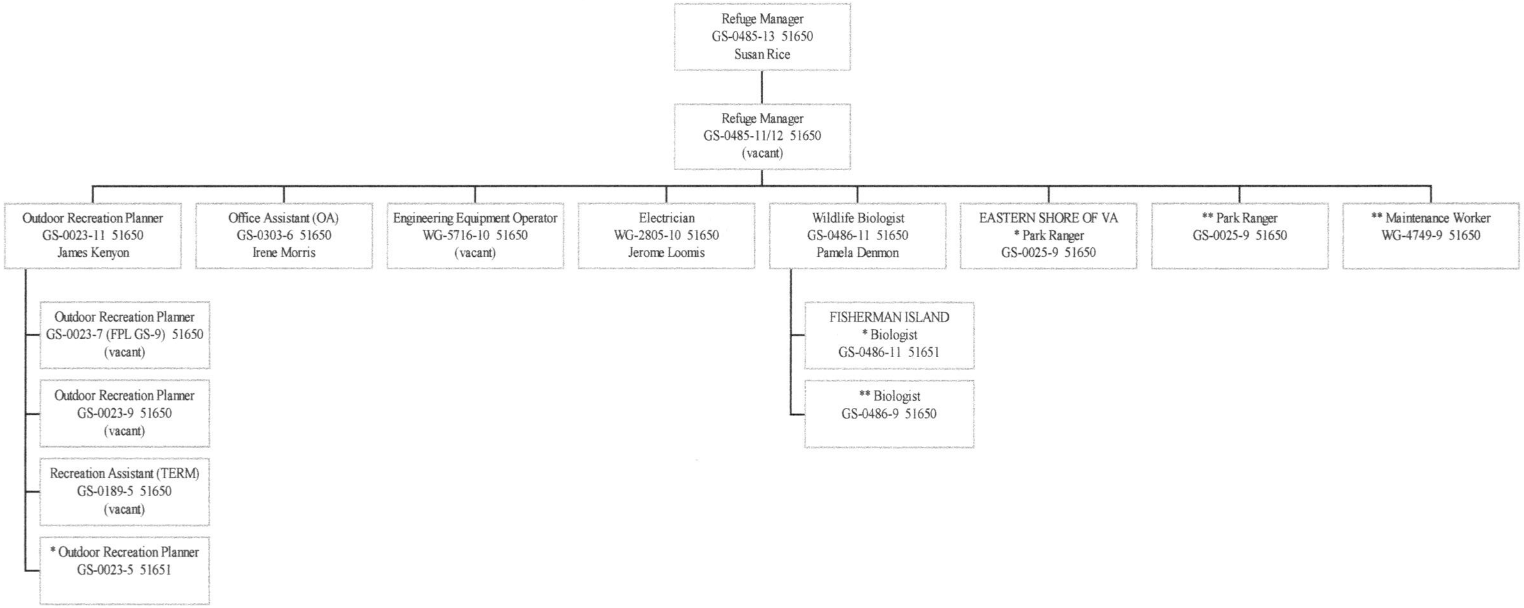

Refuge Manager
GS-0485-13 51650
Susan Rice

Refuge Manager
GS-0485-11/12 51650
(vacant)

Office Assistant (OA)
GS-0303-6 51650
Irene Morris

Engineering Equipment Operator
WG-5716-10 51650
(vacant)

Electrician
WG-2805-10 51650
Jerome Loomis

Wildlife Biologist
GS-0486-11 51650
Pamela Denmon

EASTERN SHORE OF VA
* Park Ranger
GS-0025-9 51650

** Park Ranger
GS-0025-9 51650

** Maintenance Worker
WG-4749-9 51650

Outdoor Recreation Planner
GS-0023-11 51650
James Kenyon

Outdoor Recreation Planner
GS-0023-7 (FPL GS-9) 51650
(vacant)

Outdoor Recreation Planner
GS-0023-9 51650
(vacant)

Recreation Assistant (TERM)
GS-0189-5 51650
(vacant)

* Outdoor Recreation Planner
GS-0023-5 51651

FISHERMAN ISLAND
* Biologist
GS-0486-11 51651

** Biologist
GS-0485-9 51650

_____ _____
Refuge Manager   Date

_____ _____
Regional Chief, NWRS   Date

_____ _____
Refuge Supervisor   Date

_____ _____
Regional Director   Date

* Essential Staff
** New/Expanded Staff

Eastern Shore of Virginia and Fisherman Island National Wildlife Refuges
Proposed Staffing for Alternatives B and C

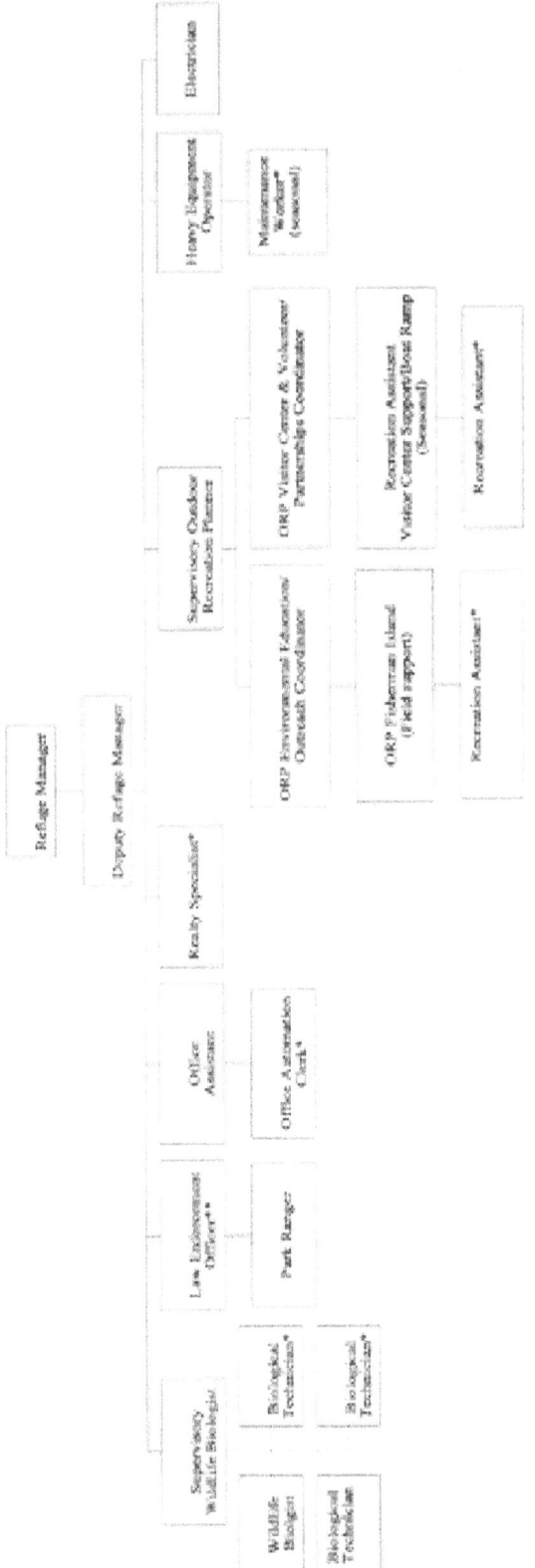

*New position proposed in CCP

**Upgraded position proposed in CCP

Appendix J

Appendix J:

Literature Cited

Adams, Matthew L. 1994. Assessment and Status of World War II Harbor Defense Structures. Submitted to Eastern Shore of Virginia National Wildlife Refuge, Cape Charles Virginia by Matthew L. Adams and Christopher K. Wiles, Ithaca, New York.

Adams, Melissa, Julia Freedgood and Jennifer Phelan. May 1999. Cost of Community Service Study for Northampton County, Virginia. American Farmland Trust: Northampton, Mass. 14 pp.

Askins, R.A. 1993. Population trends in grassland, shrubland, and forest birds in eastern North America. Pages 1-34 *in* D.M. Power, ed, Current Ornithology. Vol. 11 Plenum Publ. Corp. New York, NY.

Bailey, R.G. 1995. Description of the Ecoregions of the United States. 2nd ed. rev. and expanded (1st ed. 1980). Forest Service, U.S. Department of Agriculture. Misc. Publ. No. 1391 (rev.), pp. 31-33.

Berdeen, J. B. and D. G. Krementz. 1998. The use of fields at night by wintering American woodcock. Journal of Wildlife Management 62: 939-947.

Blake, J.G., and W. G. Hoppes. 1986. Influence of resource abundance on use of tree-fall gaps by birds in an isolated woodlot. Auk 103:328-340.

Breen, T.H. and Innes, S., 1980. "Myne Owne Ground:" Race and Freedom on Virginia's Eastern Shore, 1640-1676. Oxford University Press, New York, p. 11.

Brown, J. K. and J. K. Smith, eds. 2000. Wildland fire in ecosystems: effects of fire on flora. Gen. Tech. Rep. RMRS-GTR-42-vol. 2. Ogden, UT: U.S. Department of Agriculture, Forest Service, Rocky Mountain Research Station. 257 p.

Brown, S., C. Hickey, B. Harrington, and R. Gill, eds. 2001. The U.S. Shorebird Conservation Plan, 2nd ed. Manomet Center for Conservation Sciences, Manomet, MA.

Bureau of Economic Analysis. May 25, 2000. "BEA Regional Facts (BEARFACTS)." http://www.bea.doc.gov/bea/regional/bearfacts/index.htm.

Bureau of Economic Analysis. May 2001. Table CA25: Total full-time and part-time employment by industry, Northampton. http://www.bea.doc.gov/.

Burger, J. 1991. Foraging behavior and the effect of human disturbance on the piping plover (*Charadrius melodus*). Journal of Coastal Research 7: 39-52.

Burger, J. 1994. The effect of human disturbance on foraging behavior and habitat use in piping plover (*Charadrius melodus*). Estuaries 17: 695-701.

Costanzo, Gary. June 2001. Personal Communication.

Defenders of Wildlife. October 1998. Science-based Stewardship: Recommendations for Implementing the National Wildlife Refuge System Improvement Act. Washington, D.C.

Denmon, P. 1998. Early successional habitat use by nongame wildlife species in American woodcock breeding habitat in West Virginia. Thesis, West Virginia University, Morgantown, West Virginia, USA.

Dunn J., and K. Garrett. 1997. Warblers - Peterson Field Guides. Houghton Mifflin Company, Boston, MA. p.6

Eastern Shore of Virginia Economic Development Commission. 2000. "Eastern Shore of Virginia." http://www.easternshore.org/index.html.

Goodwin, R. Christopher, April M. Fehr and Leslie McFaden. 1989. Archaeological Reconnaissance of the Eastern Shore of Virginia National Wildlife Refuge. Northampton County, Virginia. Submitted to U.S. Fish and Wildlife Service, Region 5 by R. Christopher Goodwin and Associates. Frederick, Maryland.

Gaba, Jeffrey M. 1994. Environmental Law. West Publishing Co.: St. Paul, Minn.

Gutzwiller, Kevin J. Elizabeth A. Kroese, Stanley H. Anderson, and Charles A. Wilkins. 1997. Does human intrusion alter the seasonal timing of avian song during breeding periods? *The Auk.* 114(1):55-65.

Hagan, J.M.,III, T.L. Lloyd-Evans, J.L. Atwood, and D.S. Woods. 1992. Long-term changes in migratory landbirds in the northeastern United States: Evidence from migration capture data. pp. 115-130 in J.M. Hagan, III and D.W. Johnston, eds. Ecology and conservation of Neotropical migrant landbirds. Smithsonian Institution Press, Washington, DC.

Hecht, Anne. 2001. Personal communication.

Hodnett, E. L. 1998. Cape Charles Raptor Research Station 1998. Final Report, United States Fish and Wildlife Service. p. 7.

Kenyon, James. August 7, 2000. Personal communication.

Kenyon, James. June 18, 2001. Personal communication

Knisley, C.B. March 27, 2001. Personal communication.

Knisley C.B. and Hill J., 1999. A Survey of the Eastern Shore Of Virginia for The Northeastern Beach Tiger Beetle, *Cincindela Dorsalis Dorsalis*, 1999. Final Report. U. S. Fish and Wildlife Service. p. 7.

Krementz, D. G., and J. J. Jackson. 1999. Woodcock in the southeast: natural history and management for landowners. The University of Georgia College of Agricultural and Environmental Sciences, Cooperative Extension Service. Bulletin 1183.

The Louis Berger Group, Inc. 2000. Chesapeake Bay Bridge-Tunnel Toll Impact Study. Major Topic Reports. 16 pp. http://www.esva.net/.

Lukei, Jr., R.F. 2000. Trapping and Banding of Raptors, Eastern Shore of Virginia National Wildlife Refuge, Sep. 99 - Dec. 99. Final Report, United States Fish and Wildlife Service. p. 6.

Mallett, Steve. February 14, 2001. Personal Communication.

Manville, Albert M. 2 December 1999. The ABC's of Avoiding Bird Collisions at Communication Towers: The Next Steps. Proc. Of Avian Interactions Workshop. Charleston, SC. Arlington, VA.

Mabey, S., J. McCann, L. Niles, C. Bartlett, P. Kerlinger. August 1993. The Neotropical Migratory Songbird Coastal Corridor Study. Final Report, Virginia Department of Environmental Quality, Coastal Resources Management Program. p. 9.

Mata, L. 1997. Aerial Photographic Analysis-Fort John Custis/Cape Charles Air Force Station Study Area. Final Report, United States Environmental Protection Agency, pp. 17-25.

Mayne, Karen. No date. Water and Air Research Report Summary: Cultural Resources Survey of the Cape Charles Air Force Station and Vicinity. Submitted to the U. S. Navy in 1983 by Water and Air Research.

McGowan, James M. May 16, 2000. Personal Communication.

Mitchell, J.C. 1999. Checklist and Keys to the Amphibians and Reptiles of Virginia's Eastern Shore. Catesbeiana. 19(1): 3-4.

Mitchell, Michael. June 19, 2001. Personal Communication.

Oertel, G. 1999. Water Resources and Vegetation Patterns on Fisherman Island. Final Report, United States Fish and Wildlife Service. Coastal Bay and Barrier Island Program, Old Dominion University. pp. 10-11, 16-20.

Parrish, J. D. 1997. Patterns of frugivory and energetic condition in Neartic landbirds during autumn migration. Condor 99:681-697.

Paxton, B. J. and B. D. Watts. 2000. Investigation of grassland/shrubland migrants on the lower Delmarva Peninsula. Center for Conservation Biology Technical Report, CCBTR-00-03. College of William and Mary, Williamsburg, VA. 23pp.

Pettry, D.E., J.H. Scott, Jr., and D.J. Bliley. 1979. Distribution and nature of Carolina bays on the Eastern Shore of Virginia. Virginia Journal of Science 30: 3-9.

Pfister, C., B. A. Harrington, and M. Lavine. 1992. The impact of human disturbance on shorebirds at a migration staging area. Biological Conservation 60:115-126.

Riffell, Samuel K. Kevin J. Gutzwiller, and Stanley H. Anderson. 1996. Does repeated human intrusion cause cumulative declines in avian richness and abundance? *Ecological Applications*. 6(2). pp. 492-505.

Roble, S.M. 2001. Natural Heritage Resources of Virginia: Rare Animal Species. Natural Heritage Technical Report 01-16. Virginia Department of Conservation and Recreation, Division of Natural Heritage, Richmond, Virginia. 33 pp.

Rosenberg, K.V., et al. 1999. A land managers guide to improving habitat for scarlet tanagers and other forest-interior birds. The Cornell Lab of Ornithology.

Sample, D. W., and M. J. Mossman. 1997. Managing habitat for grassland birds: a guide for Wisconsin. Wisconsin Department of Natural Resources Publication No. SS-925-97.

Sauer, J. R., J. E. Hines, I. Thomas, J. Fallon, and G. Gough. 2000. The North American Breeding Bird Survey, Results and Analysis 1966 - 1999. Version 98.1, USGS Patuxent Wildlife Research Center, Laurel, MD.

Smith, J. K., ed. 2000. Wildland fire in ecosystems: effects of fire on fauna. Gen. Tech. Rep. RMRS-GTR-42-vol. 1. Ogden, UT: U.S. Department of Agriculture, Forest Service, Rocky Mountain Research Station. 83 p.

Spady, Denard. June 6, 2000. Personal Communication.

Struthers, H. B., J. M. Bickal, and P. G. Rodewald. 2000. Use of successional habitat and fruit resources by songbirds during autumn migration in central New Jersey. Wilson Bulletin 112:249-260.

Terwilliger, K. and B. Cross. 1999. Virginia Plover Survey: Piping Plover Productivity Studies 1999. Final Report submitted to the Virginia Dept. of Game and Inland Fisheries. 25 pp.

Terwilliger, Karen. July 18, 2000. Personal Communication.

Terwilliger, Karen. 2001. Personal communication with Pamela Denmon.

Townsend, J.F. 2001. Natural Heritage Resources of Virginia: Rare and Vascular Plants. Natural Heritage Technical Report 01-11. Virginia Department of Conservation and Recreation, Division of Natural Heritage, Richmond, Virginia. Unpublished Report. March 2001. 30 pp plus appendices.

Truitt, Barry. April 16, 2000. Personal Communication.

Tu, M., Hurd, C., & J.M. Randall, 2001. Weed Control Methods Handbook, The Nature Conservancy, http://tncweeds.ucdavis.edu, Version: April 2001.

U.S. Census Bureau. 2000. State and County QuickFacts. Http://quickfacts.census.gov/.

U.S. Department of Commerce. 1981. 1978 Census of Agriculture. Vol. 1, Part 46: Virginia state and county data. U. S. Government Printing Office. Washington, DC.

U.S. Department of Transportation and U.S. Coast Guard, Fifth Coast Guard District. October 1994. "Parallel Crossing of Chesapeake Bay. U.S. 13. Virginia Beach-Northampton County Virginia: Final Environmental Impact/4(f) Statement."

U.S. Environmental Protection Agency. May 6, 1998. Modified Site Inspection Narrative Report - Cape Charles Air Force Station Site, Cape Charles, Northampton County, Virginia. Prepared by Weston for EPA, Federal Facilities Section Philadelphia, PA.

U.S. Fish and Wildlife Service. March 1982. Refuge Manual. 3:1.1, 1.6B

U.S. Fish and Wildlife Service. October 1984. Final Environmental Assessment: Proposal to Protect Migratory Bird Habitat. Northampton County, Virginia. Fish and Wildlife Service, Region 5: Newton Corner, Massachusetts.

U. S. Fish and Wildlife Service. 1987. A Survey of the Fitchett/Hallett Cemetery, Eastern Shore of Virginia National Wildlife Refuge, Northampton County, Virginia. Region 5, Newton, Massachusetts.

U.S. Fish and Wildlife Service. May 1988. North American Waterfowl Management Plan: Atlantic Coast Joint Venture. 106 pp.

U.S. Fish and Wildlife Service. October 1990. Regional Wetlands Concept Plan: Emergency Wetlands Resources Act, Northeast Region. Newton Corner, Massachusetts. 18 pp.

U.S. Fish and Wildlife Service. 1993a. Delmarva Fox Squirrel (Sciurus niger cinereus) Recovery Plan, Second Revision. Hadley, Massachusetts. 104 pp.

U.S. Fish and Wildlife Service. 1993b. Eastern Shore of Virginia National Wildlife Refuge Hunt Plan. 12 pp. plus appendices.

U.S. Fish and Wildlife Service. 1994a. Northeastern Beach Tiger Beetle (*Cincindela dorsalis dorsalis* Say) Recover Plan. Hadley, Massachusetts. 60 pp.

U.S. Fish and Wildlife Service. 1994b. Final Corrective Action Plan and Preliminary Assessment for Eastern Shore of VA NWR, Cape Charles, VA. USFWS, Engineering Services Division, Lakewood CO.

U.S. Fish and Wildlife Service. May 1996a. Delaware River/Delmarva Coastal Watershed Team Plan. Hadley, Massachusetts. 26 pp.

U.S. Fish and Wildlife Service. 1996b. Piping Plover (*haradrius melodus*) Atlantic Coast Population, Revised Recovery Plan. Hadley, Massachusetts. 245 pp.

U.S. Fish and Wildlife Service. 1996c. Recovery Plan for Seabeach amaranth (Amaranthus pumilus) Rafinesque. Atlanta, Georgia. 65 pp.

U.S. Fish and Wildlife Service. May 1997a. Chesapeake Bay/Susquehanna River Ecosystem Team Plan. Hadley, Massachusetts. 16 pp.

U.S Fish and Wildlife Service. July 1997b. Banking on Nature: The Economic Benefits to Local Communities of National Wildlife Refuge Visitation. Prepared by Andrew Laughland and James Caudill. 118 pp.

U.S. Fish and Wildlife Service. March 22, 1999a. Fulfilling the Promise: The National Wildlife Refuge System. Visions for Wildlife, Habitat, People, and Leadership.

U.S. Fish and Wildlife Service. April 1999b. Partners in Flight: Mid-Atlantic Coastal Plain Bird Conservation Plan (Physiographic Area #44). Hadley, Massachusetts. 81 pp. (Draft)

U.S. Fish and Wildlife Service. December 2000. Rhode Island National Wildlife Refuge Complex Draft Comprehensive Conservation Plan and Environmental Assessment. Hadley, MA.

U.S. Fish and Wildlife Service. 2000a. 1999 status update: U.S. Atlantic Coast piping plover population. Sudbury, Massachusetts. 8 pp. Http://pipingplover.fws.gov/status/.

U.S. Fish and Wildlife Service. March 2001a. Final CAP Report for Eastern Shore Of Virginia NWR. https://ecos.fws.gov/ecapreport/final_report.html. Gloucester, Virginia.

U.S. Fish and Wildlife Service. April 2001b. Final CAP Report for Fisherman Island NWR. Https://ecos.fws.gov/ecapreport/final-report.html. Gloucester, Virginia.

Vickery, P.D, M.I. Hunter, Jr., and S. M. Melvin. 1994. Effects of habitat area on the distribution of grassland birds in Maine. Conservation Biology 8:1087-1097.

Virant II, Leo B. 1975. Memorandum for Record, Subject: Historical Survey of Fort John Custis. TRADOC ODCSRM-MPD/4446. Fort Monroe, Virginia.

Virginia Tourism Corporation. Virginia Travel 2000: Summarizes the year-to-date travel data for 2000. Virginia Tourism Corporation. http://www.vatc.org/research/files/2000trav.doc.

Watts, B.D., D. S. Bradshaw, and K. Terwilliger. Undated. Dune stability and piping plover distribution along the Virginia barrier islands. Draft ms., College of William and Mary.

Watts, B. November 2000. Personal Communication.

Watts, B.D., and S.E. Mabey. 1994. Migratory landbirds on the lower Delmarva: Habitat selection and geographic distribution. Final report for NOAA.

Weir, R.D., et al. 1980. Fall migration of Saw-whet Owls at Prince Edward Point, Ontario. Wilson Bull. 92(4):475-488.

Wesler, K.W., D.J. Pogue, A.F. Button, G.J. Fine, P.A. Sternheimer, and E.G. Ferguson 1981. The M/DOT Archeological Resources Survey Volume 1: Eastern Shore. Maryland Historical Trust Manuscript Series, Num. 7, p. 431.

Wilbur Smith Associates. July 1999. U.S. Route 13 Corridor Plan: Eastern Shore of Virginia. Shore Engineering. Fitzgerald & Halliday, Inc.

Appendix K

Appendix K:
Draft Land Protection Plan

Draft Land Protection Plan
Eastern Shore of Virginia National Wildlife Refuge

I. Introduction

This Draft Land Protection Plan (LPP) identifies an expanded acquisition area for the Eastern Shore of Virginia National Wildlife Refuge (NWR), as proposed in our attached Comprehensive Conservation Plan (CCP) for the refuge (Alternative B: The Service's Proposed Action, draft CCP/EA).[1] The purpose of this LPP is to

- provide landowners and the public with an outline of U.S. Fish and Wildlife Service (Service, we, our) policies, priorities and potential protection methods for lands within the project area.

- assist landowners with determining whether or not their property is within the proposed boundary.

- inform landowners about our long-standing policy of acquiring land only from willing sellers. [No purchase of land or easement will occur if an owner is not interested in selling.]

The LPP presents methods that the Service and interested landowners can use to accomplish wildlife habitat objectives within the proposed boundary. Maps and a table with ownership information are included to help landowners understand our interest in conservation of these lands.

The maps (Appendix A) show the existing refuge, our proposed acquisition boundary, and the land parcels within this area. A corresponding table identifies each parcel, its tax map number, acreage, ownership, and our priority and recommended option for habitat protection.

Lands or conservation easements acquired will be managed to provide critical stopover habitat, in support of the millions of birds that funnel through this key migration site. Some lands may also be managed for threatened and endangered species, or to maintain significant natural resources such as wetlands and related wildlife, or to provide public use opportunities. We propose to develop cooperative management agreements with State agency partners responsible for conservation lands in the project area.

II. Project Description

Existing Refuge
The refuge is located on the southern tip of the Delmarva Peninsula in Northampton County, Virginia, at the mouth of the Chesapeake Bay (Bay). Currently, the refuge consists of 1,121 acres, including deciduous and evergreen forest, myrtle and bayberry thicket, grassland, ponds with associated fresh marsh, tidal salt marsh and beach habitats. It was established in 1984 through a transfer of excess military land, the former Cape Charles Air Force Station, for the following purposes:

- to conserve, manage and enhance habitat for use by endangered and threatened species, migratory birds and other species of fish and wildlife.
- to encourage a natural diversity of habitat and associated fish and wildlife species.
- to fulfill the international treaty obligations of the United States relating to fish and wildlife.
- to provide fish and wildlife-oriented recreation and education.

Recent land acquisition activities have included:

- purchase of the Wise Point Corporation property (376 acres, 2001), located within the acquisition boundary approved for the refuge in 1984;
- donation of two properties as mitigation for refuge habitat lost to bridge construction,

---

[1] USFWS Region 5 Eastern Shore of Virginia and Fisherman Island National Wildlife Refuges Draft Comprehensive Conservation Plan and Environmental Assessment (Hadley, Massachusetts: March 2003).

added to the refuge as Categorical Exclusions under National Environmental Policy Act procedures. The first is an agricultural parcel (74 acres, 1995) directly north of the visitor center, which is being restored to wildlife habitat;

- the second is a 2 ½-mile section of the 66'-wide abandoned railroad right-of-way (20 acres, 1997), from the refuge to Cedar Grove.

The existing acquisition boundary approved in 1984 included 1,337 acres (estimate, not surveyed acres). There are four remaining unacquired parcels within this original boundary (310 acres): one private ownership (160 acres, Holly Bluff Island), Northampton County ownership (60 acres, Raccoon Park), a tract of state-owned marsh between the two (approximately 89 acres), and a small electrical substation tract (1 acre) owned by Eastern Shore Public Service Company of Virginia. Although within the original boundary, the four parcels are incorporated into this proposal and listed as the first four tracts in the table.

Proposed Expansion
Within the mid-Atlantic Region, the lower Cape May and Delmarva (Cape Charles) peninsulas are the most significant bird migration bottlenecks known, concentrating large numbers of migrants at their southern tips. Stopover habitats at these points are critical to fall migration, and are considered some of the highest conservation priorities in eastern North America.

Due to geographic configuration, the lower Delmarva peninsula provides critical habitat for large concentrations of raptors, songbirds, other migrant landbirds, shorebirds, woodcock, and waterfowl. The southern tip has been designated an Important Bird Area by the American Bird Conservancy / National Audubon Society, in conjunction with the Partners-In-Flight (PIF) program. Many of these in-transit migrants are PIF priority species breeding in physiographic areas / Bird Conservation Regions throughout the northeast. Protection of habitat at this key stopover site is critical to the conservation of both temperate and neotropical migratory birds.

The importance of the area is also reflected in the following designations for the surrounding barrier island / marsh-lagoon system: North American Waterfowl Management Plan focus area (Atlantic Coast Joint Venture); Western Hemisphere Shorebird Reserve Network site; United Nations Bioshpere Reserve and National Natural Landmark (TNC Virginia Coast Reserve); RAMSAR site (Chesapeake Bay); Emergency Wetlands Resources Act priority site (Regional Wetlands Concept Plan). The lower county was designated as a Special Area Management Plan site, with funding and support from Virginia's Coastal Program and NOAA, which have supported several bird studies.

A primary purpose of the refuge, situated at the tip, is to provide habitat for migrants. Several studies, including the 4-state Neotropical Migratory Songbird Coastal Corridor Study, have identified habitat protection in the vicinity of the refuge as a critical need. They show that the highest concentrations of migrants occur within a 10 kilometer (6.2 miles) zone closest to the tip, in a 1.5 km wide strip (0.9 mi) bordering bayside and seaside coastlines. Because of the concentration effect, protection or restoration of habitat of any size or configuration within this "10 km zone" is important.

This LPP identifies a 6,030-acre acquisition area for the refuge, based on the 10-km zone, which will allow the Service to protect or restore additional migration habitat within the critical area of the southern tip. This will be accomplished through the acquisition of lands, conservation easements, or development of cooperative agreements.

The proposed acquisition area also provides important breeding and wintering habitat, and supports species of concern at both the federal and state levels, including the Bald eagle (Elliott's Creek area) and northeastern beach tiger beetle (Bay beaches).

III. Status of Resources to be Protected

Although most of the Eastern Shore's barrier island and marsh system is protected, studies and experts agree on the urgent need for protection of critical forested and shrub migration habitat at the southern tip.

Historically, Northampton County has been a rural community with agriculture and seafood providing the basis of the economy. Cropland and woodland are the predominant land covertypes within the proposed refuge expansion boundary, occupying 62% and 34% respectively of the land area (tidal marsh excluded) within the boundary.

Until recent times, the area had remained a relatively isolated rural agricultural area because of limited access. Construction of the Chesapeake Bay Bridge linking Washington/ Baltimore with the Delmarva Peninsula, and the Chesapeake Bay Bridge-Tunnel (CBBT), linking Hampton Roads with the lower peninsula in 1964, increased the accessibility and exposure of the area. The Chesapeake Bay Bridge-Tunnel District recently completed a second bridge crossing (1998), and implemented a 24-hour round trip commuter toll (2002).

According to the recent Toll Impact Study, annual traffic on the CBBT has nearly tripled since its opening in 1964, and total traffic has increased nearly 15 percent since 1990. This trend is expected to continue, with through traffic predicted to double through 2020.

These changes have resulted in a marked recent increase in development pressure in the southern tip area. Low land prices, access to the Bay and ocean, and proximity to major population centers (Washington/Baltimore, Philadelphia/New Jersey and Norfolk/Tidewater) have drawn attention to the area by investors, second-home buyers, and retirees. Large land parcels in the vicinity of the refuge are now rapidly being subdivided and/or developed.

We recognize previous land use patterns and stewardship by local landowners as having maintained the unique wildlife values of this area in the past. However, farms and family lands, previously maintained as larger rural parcels compatible with wildlife use and public access, are slowly being subdivided and developed.

This situation is resulting in a cumulative loss of important forested and shrub migration habitats and further fragmentation. Opportunities for restoring these habitats from agricultural lands, at the critical southern tip, will also be lost. Loss of stopover habitat at concentration sites such as this will likely result in irreversible negative impacts to neotropical and short distance migrant species, many of which are identified as Partners-in-Flight priorities.

According to the Toll Impact Study, real estate experts have suggested that the price of bayfront property has tripled over the past two to three years, sold to second home buyers, retirees and investors. Other comments were made that the county experienced the highest level of market activity (land sales) in its history in 2000, and that there are few bayfront properties left on the market. The effects of the toll discount are likely to be long-term induced development. The toll study predicts that increases in tourism, second home development, and full-time residential population will impact carrying capacity of schools, aquifers, septic and sewer systems, road facilities and land resources.

IV. Proposed Action and Objectives

The Service will acquire lands or conservation easements from willing sellers, within the 6,030-acre proposed acquisition boundary. These lands will be managed as part of the Eastern Shore of Virginia NWR, as discussed in the attached CCP. Cooperative management agreements will be used in some cases.

Our objectives are:

- Protect existing forest and shrub migration habitat, located within the southern 10 km of the peninsula, identified as critical to migrant landbirds.

- Restore forest and shrub habitat from agricultural lands within this same area, to widen/reconnect the vegetated migration corridor (particularly along the bayside).
- Restore several large grassland tracts from agricultural lands as opportunities occur, to provide migration, breeding and wintering habitat for declining grassland bird species.
- Protect known sites of threatened or endangered species and rare natural communities (e.g., Bald eagle and tiger beetle nesting sites).

Acquisition of lands in the proposal area will prevent significant loss of important habitat, and allow restoration of additional habitat necessary to support large concentrations of migratory birds.

Proposed Acquisition Area
The proposed acquisition area is based upon the 10km zone identified as critical to migrants. The boundary has been adjusted to correspond to property boundaries and identifiable features, such as roads. It extends from the tip of the peninsula north along the Chesapeake Bay shoreline to Plantation Creek, and north along the seaside shoreline up to Walls Landing Creek, just south of Capeville. It is bounded along the bayside by Route 645, and along the seaside by Route 600.

We are not interested in acquiring developed lands in the vicinity of villages or subdivisions. Our interest is to protect and restore wildlife habitat. Therefore, certain lands have been excluded from the refuge acquisition area. These are the rural village districts, as designated by Northampton County, including Cedar Grove, Magotha, Townsend, Capeville, and Cheapside. Also excluded are the bayshore subdivisions of Latimer's Bluff, Butler's Bluff, Bay Ridge, Guy's Landing, Elliott's Creek, Sugar Hill, Chesapeake Shores and Arlington Plantation.

In addition to the refuge, other conservation lands exist in the vicinity of the southern tip, including Kiptopeke State Park (535 acres), the GATR Tract (356 acres, part of the state's Mockhorn Wildlife Management Area), and the Trower Natural Area Preserve (35 acres). These lands are not included in the refuge acquisition area. However, we are proposing to develop cooperative management agreements with the agencies responsible for these lands, to acknowledge a common goal of providing habitat for migrants. The agencies include the Department of Conservation and Recreation, both the Divisions of State Parks and Natural Heritage, and the Department of Game and Inland Fisheries.

Land Cover / Land Use
The majority of the lands included within the proposed acquisition area are undeveloped forest, farmland, and wetland. General land cover, land use, and wetland types within the proposed acquisition area are summarized in Tables 1 and 2. Forested habitats are dominated by mixed hardwoods and loblolly pine, with an associated shrub understory. These habitats are important to migrants. Of the approximately 1,810 acres of forest within the proposal, 460 acres are forested wetland. Over half of the land is agricultural cropland, 55%. These lands represent the potential to restore needed habitat within this critical geographic area.

Table 1.—General land use / land cover categories within the proposed acquisition boundary

Land cover / land use	Acres	%
Forested	1,810	30
Agricultural	3,315	55
Tidal Marsh	725	12
Open Water	120	2
Other	62	1
Total	6,032	100

Table 2.—Wetland habitats within the proposed acquisition area

Wetland type	Acres	%
Forested wetland	460	8
Tidal Marsh	725	12
Open Water	120	2
Shrub/freshwater marsh/meadow	25	<1
Total	1,330	23

Maps and Ownership Table

Maps and a table listing all land parcels are provided in Appendix A. Both maps and table were produced using Northampton County tax parcel boundaries and tax database information. These are provided to inform landowners of our interest in lands within this area.

Each parcel is identified on the maps with a number which is keyed to the table, listed in the first column as LPP number (LPP NO.). The following information is provided in the table:

- Northampton County tax map, or "insert" number
- County tax parcel number
- Owner's last name
- Acreage of the parcel
- Service priority for acquisition - the importance of the parcel to the project
- Proposed acquisition or protection method
- Zoning designation

Land Protection Priorities

As land parcels within the proposed acquisition area are offered to the Service, and as funds become available, acquisition priority will be based on habitat type and location, as follows:

Priority 1: Parcels with significant (over 1 acre) tracts of existing forested or shrub migration habitat, located at the southern tip (from Cedar Grove south) and along the bayside shoreline (between the bayshore and Route 645, north to Plantation Creek). This area supports

higher densities of high-volume migrants than the seaside (approximately 3:1) for two main reasons: 1) greater forest and shrub understory diversity, producing more food, and 2) a "reverse migration" phenomenon causing re-distribution of migrants into bayside habitats. In addition, this is a high priority because the threat of habitat loss to subdivision and development is more immediate.

Priority 2: Parcels with significant (over 1 acre) tracts of existing forested or shrub migration habitat, located along the seaside coastline (between the seaside coastline and Route 600, from Cedar Grove north to Walls Landing Creek). While still within the critical lower 10k area, bird densities are not as high as on the bayside. Also, due to topography, this side of the peninsula supports more extensive forested/shrub wetland transition zone grading into tidal marsh, and offers greater opportunity for wetland and riparian buffer restoration.

Priority 3: Parcels that consist of predominantly agricultural land with no existing forest or shrub (less than an acre) and no coastal connection. Although unvegetated, these lands are important because they offer the opportunity to restore migration habitat within the 10km geographic area. Such opportunities are important to attempt to offset future habitat losses to subdivision and development within this area.

Priority 4: Those relatively small parcels, generally less than 5 acres, that include collections of buildings such as residences, farm houses, barns, various tractor and equipment sheds, farm storage or processing buildings. Our intention is not to acquire residences and buildings, but to protect or restore habitat, so these parcels will be evaluated on a case-by-case basis.

Table 3 presents a summary by method and priority. See Appendix A for the details on each parcel. The CCP will incorporate our approved final LPP as a management action in support of land protection goals and objectives.

Table 3.—Acquisition Area Summary, by Method and Priority

Priority	Method	Acres	Parcels
1	Cooperative Agreement	122	2
1	Fee	1	1
1	Easement	41	1
1	Fee or Easement	4,743	84
2	Fee or Easement	668	18
3	Fee or Easement	424	42
4	Fee	33	21
Total		**6,032**	**169**

V. Protection Options

The following protection options were considered in the development of our proposed action, presented in detail in Appendix A. They include:

- no Service action
- management or acquisition by others
- less-than-fee acquisition by the Service
- fee acquisition by the Service

Service land protection policy is to acquire only the minimum interest necessary to meet the refuge's goals and objectives, and only from willing sellers.

We are proposing varying levels of Service action within the project area. A combination of the protection options outlined below will be used, including assistance and support to conservation partners and landowners, acquisition and management by others, and purchase of lands or conservation easements by the Service.

We believe this combination approach is a cost-effective way of providing the minimal level of protection needed to accomplish project objectives, while also attempting to meet the needs of landowners. As parcels become available in the future, however, changes in the protection option for a specific parcel may be warranted to ensure

we are using the option that best fits the situation at that time.

Option 1.—No Action

Under Option 1, we would maintain present refuge acquisition boundaries; we would not expand the refuge or otherwise attempt to protect additional migration habitat. Our draft CCP/EA evaluates this option as "Alternative A: No Action (Current Management)." We did not select this approach as our proposed action because:

- It will not adequately protect important migration habitat, Bald eagle and tiger beetle nesting sites, and wetland habitat in the project area;
- Service action has been recommended and supported by our State and non-profit conservation partners, as part of a cooperative effort.

Regulatory land use controls do exist for the area, including county zoning and Chesapeake Bay Preservation Act restrictions. The County's Comprehensive Plan reflects local support of the area's natural resources (including migratory birds), seen as vital to the community's economic well being. Because of accelerating development pressures, a proposed new zoning overlay, called the Southern Tip Rural District, is currently under consideration to help protect sensitive natural areas, vegetative cover, and habitat.

However, much of the project area is highly developable upland, either forestland or prime agricultural soils. Further subdivision, forest clearing, and residential development is allowable within the proposed 6,032-acre acquisition area under current zoning regulations. Zoning within the area is as follows:

Zoning Designation	Acres	%
Agricultural	3,406	56
Agricultural / Forestal District	1,650	27
Rural Village District	936	16
Existing Business Commercial Waterfront	41	< 1

The majority of lands within the project area, over 83 percent, are zoned Agricultural (A-1) and Agricultural/Forestal District (AFD). While the county does place importance upon preserving prime agricultural soils and woodland, the Agricultural zoning allows an overall residential density of one unit per 20 acres. Sliding scale "bonus" lots of 20,000 square feet may be divided from parcels, based on buildable area, with parcels as small as 7 acres possibly supporting 2 lots.

The Agricultural/Forestal District is an overlay district intended to support continued agricultural and forestry use through reduced-tax status. Lands can be removed from the program for subdivision and development, however, with payment of back taxes.

The Chesapeake Bay Preservation Act (1988) provides for protection of high-quality state waters, through pollution reduction regulations and development restrictions within designated Resource Protection Areas. These include shoreline, tidal wetlands, and 100-foot buffer zones. Northampton County also applies this status to the seaside, and adjacent Resource Management Areas have been designated. In reality, development or clearing of shorelands has continued throughout the state under these designations, which have not been strictly enforced with variances often granted.

The lower peninsula is presently threatened by rapid commercial and residential development which, in its present form, is incompatible with the maintenance of vegetated stopover habitat. Large tracts within the project boundary are being subdivided or developed, resulting in a cumulative loss of key habitats.

The October 2001 Chesapeake Bay Bridge-Tunnel Commuter Toll Impact Study projected that the lower third of the County would attract 70 percent of the new residential and commercial growth induced by reductions in the Bridge toll. As a result, up to 45% of the undeveloped land in this part of the county will be permanently converted if no action is taken.

The study estimated that new development could eventually occupy up to 10,536 acres of farmland and forests. The bayside tracts most critical to migratory songbirds are already being subdivided at a rapid pace, and land prices have escalated since implementation of the commuter toll, March 2002 .

Option 2.—Management or Acquisition by Others

Under Option 2, we would continue to support the activities of our partner organizations and agencies within the project area, such as the Virginia Department of Game and Inland Fisheries, the Virginia Department of Conservation and Recreation (DCR), the Virginia Natural Heritage Program, the Virginia Coastal Program, The Nature Conservancy, the USDA

Natural Resource Conservation Service, and interested local landowners.

Recent support provided by the Service for land protection projects in Northampton County has included: a $798,000 National Coastal Wetland Grant for the conservation component of the county's Sustainable Technologies Park; similar grants to Virginia DCR's Division of Natural Heritage for Savage Neck and TNC for Elkins Marsh; and active support and participation in the addition of the Parsons property to Kiptopeke State Park. TNC and the Trust for Public Lands have historically provided land acquisition support to the refuge.

Although our partners provide land with some level of protection, they often do not have the financial or administrative resources to buy all those lands, nor can they always actively manage the parcels to protect our priority species. The proposed action (Appendix A) assumes these groups will continue to buy lands in the project area, subject to their own funding limitations. However, without our contribution to land protection, many lands identified as important to wildlife would likely be converted to other uses. The collective partnership effort has identified a Service acquisition and management role as critical to long-term protection of these significant natural resources.

While the Service already has a cooperative management agreement in place for the county's Raccoon Park tract adjacent to the refuge, we propose to develop similar cooperative agreements with: 1) the Department of Conservation and Recreation for Kiptopeke State Park; 2) the Department of Game and Inland Fisheries, for the Mockhorn Wildlife Management Area tract north of the refuge, and a marsh tract within the acquisition boundary south of the refuge (LPP tract 1); and 3) the Virginia DCR Division of Natural Heritage for the Trower Natural Area Preserve. We can agree to work together to complement each other's management approaches and activities, to the extent possible, in support of the area's migratory bird resources.

Option 3.—Less–than–fee Acquisition

Under Option 3, we would accomplish our habitat objectives by purchasing only a partial interest, a conservation easement. The parcel would remain in private ownership, while allowing us some ability to manage land use. The easement would be structured to assure the permanent protection of existing forested and shrub habitat, allow habitat management/improvement, manage access if endangered or threatened species are present, and possibly provide limited public use opportunities if the landowner is willing.

In order to accomplish these objectives, we would purchase the development and timber rights, and possibly access or hunting rights. Easements are property rights and are usually perpetual. If a landowner sells his/her property after selling an easement to us, the easement continues as part of the title. Properties subject to easements generally remain on the tax roll, although the assessment may be reduced by the reduction of market value. The Service does not make revenue-sharing payments for easement rights.

In general, an easement would maintain the land in its current configuration with no further subdivision. Easements are appropriate for use where:

- Only minimal management of the resource is needed, such as in places where the management objective is to allow forest to remain and provide habitat for migratory and resident songbirds;
- A landowner is interested in maintaining ownership of the land, does not want it to be further developed, and would like to realize the financial benefits of selling development and timber rights.

For parcels with lands in agriculture, the landowner could retain agricultural rights and continue farming, or sell those rights to us. In the latter case we would restore the farmland to vegetated habitat over time.

Determination of value for purchase of a conservation easement involves an appraisal of the rights to be purchased, based on recent market conditions in the area.

Option 4.—Fee Acquisition

Under Option 4, we would acquire parcels in fee title from willing sellers, thereby purchasing all rights of ownership. Fee ownership will assure the permanent protection of existing forested and shrub migration habitat, and allow refuge staff to:

- conduct activities such as habitat management/ improvement,
- provide public use opportunities and manage access,
- and manage for endangered or threatened species.

Fee purchase, at market value, is the most expensive method but allows the Service maximum management flexibility. This method would allow us to conduct active habitat improvement projects, such as thinning of dense pine overstory to promote understory shrub growth for migrants, and invasive plant management in general. It would allow the greatest ability for the refuge to provide additional public use opportunities. It would also provide the opportunity to restore some agricultural lands to forest and shrub, within this critical stopover area.

In most cases, for privately-owned parcels within the proposed boundary that contain tracts of forest critical to migrants, either fee purchase or conservation easements could accomplish our habitat protection objectives. Both are listed in appendix A interchangeably as options, to better meet the needs of landowners.

It may become necessary in the future to convert a conservation easement to fee acquisition. For example, when an owner is interested in selling the remainder of interest in the land. We will evaluate this need on a case-by-case basis.

Options Considered but Dismissed

We considered the action of leasing farmlands to restore migration habitat, such as possibly "resting" farm fields and rotating them out of production for a number of years to provide grassland habitat for birds. A lease would be a short-term (usually 5 to 10 years) agreement for full or specified use in return for a rental payment (usually annual) and generally includes occupancy rights. The rights revert back to the owner at the termination of the lease. This device is useful when the objectives are short term. The property remains on the tax rolls during the term of the lease.

This method does not offer permanent long-term protection and does not appear to be cost effective, given limitations on use and amounts of funding available. However, we plan to promote and facilitate habitat restoration programs offered by the Natural Resources Conservation Service, the Farm Services Administration, and our own Partners for Wildlife program within the project area. The refuge will assist interested landowners with existing programs that provide funding, materials, and technical assistance to restore permanent riparian buffers and other vegetated habitats, such as the Conservation Reserve Program and Wetland Reserve Program.

VI. Acquisition Methods

We can use four methods of acquiring either a full or partial interest in parcels within the proposed acquisition boundary, if landowners are interested:

(1) purchase (e.g., fee title, or a partial interest like a conservation easement), (2) donations, (3) exchanges, and (4) transfers. Our proposed method has been listed in Table 1 for each tract within the refuge acquisition boundary.

Purchase

For the majority of tracts within the boundary, the proposed method is listed as **Fee** or **Easement**. For those parcels we can accomplish our objectives through either method. The method used is partly dependant on the landowner's wishes.

Fee purchase involves buying the parcel of land outright from a willing seller in fee title (all rights, complete ownership), as the availability of funding allows. Fee ownership will assure the permanent protection of existing forested and shrub migration habitat, and allow refuge staff to conduct activities such as habitat management/ improvement, provide public use opportunities and manage access, and manage for endangered or threatened species. It would also give the Service the ability to restore some agricultural lands to forest and shrub, within this critical stopover area.

Easement refers to the purchase of limited rights (less-than-fee) from an interested landowner. The landowner retains ownership of the land, and would sell certain rights to the Service, to be identified and agreed upon by both parties. Our conservation easement objectives would again be to assure the permanent protection of existing forested and shrub habitat, allow habitat management/improvement, manage access if endangered or threatened species are present, and possibly provide limited public use opportunities if the landowner is willing.

In order to accomplish these objectives, we would be willing to purchase at least the development and timber rights, and possibly the ability to control access or manage hunting. Easements are property rights and are usually perpetual. If a landowner sells his/her property, the easement continues as part of the title. Properties subject to easements generally remain on the tax rolls, although the assessment may be reduced by the reduction of market value. The Service does not make revenue-sharing payments for easement rights it owns.

Funding for Fee or Easement Purchase
Much of our funding to buy land comes from the Land and Water Conservation Fund (LWCF), which is derived from certain user fees, proceeds from the disposal of surplus Federal property, the Federal motor boat fuels tax, and oil and gas lease revenues. About 90 percent of that fund now derives from Outer Continental Shelf oil and gas leases. The Federal Government receives 40 percent of that fund to acquire and develop nationally significant lands. Another source of funding to purchase land is the Migratory Bird Conservation Fund (MBCF), which derives from Federal Duck Stamp revenue.

We plan to use both funds to buy either full or partial interests in lands within the project area. LWCF funds will be used to acquire land and easements that consist mainly of forest and agricultural fields, roughly 80% of the proposed expansion area. MBCF funds may be used for properties that include large tracts of tidal marsh or forested wetlands important to waterfowl, the remaining 20%. North American Wetland Conservation Act funding is another potential source for this latter category.

Donation

We generally encourage donations in fee title or conservation easement within the approved areas, assuming management concerns, such as contaminants, are not a major issue. Owners sometimes choose to donate all or a portion of their land because of tax advantages or as a lasting memorial. We are not currently aware of any opportunities to accept donations of parcels within our proposed boundary, but would evaluate them on a case-by-case basis as they arise.

Exchange

We have the authority to exchange land in Service ownership for other land that has greater habitat or wildlife value. Inherent in this concept is the requirement to get dollar-for-dollar value, with,

occasionally, an equalization payment. Exchanges are attractive because they usually do not increase Federal land holdings or require purchase funds; however, they also may be very labor-intensive, and take a long time to complete.

Transfer

Property can be transferred to the Service through the General Services Administration (GSA) under the Federal Property and Administrative Service Act (63 Stat. 377) and Public Law 80-537 (62 Stat. 240). The refuge was originally established in 1984 through transfer land declared excess by the military, formerly the Cape Charles Air Force Station. The only property within the proposal area for which transfer could be a potential method is the 60-acre County property within the refuge's original acquisition boundary, LPP Tract 3.

This is former Federal land, transferred to the County at no cost when the military base closed. It could be voluntarily reverted back, through the National Park Service to the General Services Administration, for transfer into the Refuge System. The Service already has a Cooperative Agreement in place with the County for management of this tract.

Service Land Acquisition Policies
Once a refuge acquisition boundary is approved we will contact landowners to determine if any are interested in selling. If a landowner expresses an interest and gives permission, a real estate appraiser will appraise the property to determine the market value. Once an appraisal is conducted, we can present an offer for the landowner's consideration.

The Service's established policy is to work with willing sellers, as funds become available. We will continue to operate under this long-standing policy. Appraisals are conducted by Service or contract appraisers and meet federal as well as professional standards. The Service is required by law to purchase properties at fair market value, based on comparable sales of similar types of properties.

The acquisition boundary is based on biological importance of key habitats, and merely gives the Service the approval to negotiate with landowners that may be interested, or become interested in the future. With internal approvals in place, the Service can react more quickly if these important lands become available. Lands within this boundary do not become part of the refuge unless sold or donated to the Service.

A landowner may choose to sell land to the Service in fee simple and retain the right to occupy an existing residence. This is referred to as a **"life-use reservation."** As the name implies, life-use reservations apply to the seller's lifetime, but they can also apply for a specific number of years. At the time we acquire the parcel, we would discount from the appraised value of the buildings and land the term of the reservation. The occupant would be responsible for the upkeep on the reserved premises. We would own the land, and make revenue-sharing payments to the County.

In rare circumstances "friendly condemnation" can be used at the request of a seller. Although the Service has a long-standing policy of acquiring land only from willing sellers, it does have the power of eminent domain, like other Federal agencies. Friendly condemnation is used when the Service and a seller cannot agree on property value, and both agree to allow a Court to determine fair market value. Or, where we cannot determine the rightful owner of a property, we may use friendly condemnation to clear title. We do not expect to use friendly condemnation very often, if at all.

VII. Coordination

The Service has participated in a loosely-organized Southern Tip Partners planning group since the mid-80's. This local partnership has promoted and facilitated protection of the area's important natural resources while encouraging sustainable economic development and eco-tourism. The group has included participation from:

Northampton County

Commonwealth of Virginia State Delegate
U.S. Representative Bateman's, Davis', and Schrock's Offices
The Nature Conservancy
Local landowner representatives
Virginia Dept. of Game and Inland Fisheries
Virginia Dept. of Conservation and Recreation
Virginia Coastal Program
The Trust for Public Lands
other invited participants/researchers/officials.

Several goals of this partnership's original 1987 plan have been accomplished, including expansion of the refuge, completion of the adjacent Fisherman Island NWR, creation of nearby Kiptopeke State Park, and establishment of a Refuge visitor center.

We continue to receive support from and work closely with the Virginia Department of Game and Inland Fisheries, the Virginia Division of Natural Heritage, Kiptopeke State Park, Virginia Tech's National Fish and Wildlife Information Exchange, the Virginia GAP Analysis Project, the Center for Conservation Biology at the College of William and Mary, the Coastal Virginia Wildlife Observatory, and other researchers. The Service's Delaware Bay Estuary Project office supported planning with its Delmarva Conservation Corridor analysis.

The Service has assisted Northampton County with its Port of Cape Charles Sustainable Technology Industrial Park, through a $798,000 National Coastal Wetlands Grant for habitat protection. This project was designated by the President's Council on Sustainable Development as the only rural of four national demonstration sites. Other National Coastal Wetlands Grants have been approved elsewhere in the county, including TNC and Division of Natural Heritage proposals.

As part of the draft CCP/EA planning process, we convened a biological workshop to gather input from experts and researchers regarding wildlife status and needs on the lower peninsula. We also held three open-house public meetings and sent out newsletters and surveys to solicit public comments on various refuge aspects and issues, including Service land acquisition. Comments regarding expansion of the refuge and protection of additional habitat were supportive.

This draft LPP will be distributed to all affected landowners, our conservation partners, County offices, and others, and made available for a public comment period. Public meetings will also be held.

VIII. Socioeconomic and Cultural Impacts

The history and culture of the Eastern Shore have been intimately tied to these migratory bird resources for generations and would be severely impacted by their loss. Ecotourism based on these avian resources has become a local growth industry. The fall migration of neotropical birds on the lower peninsula is the subject of an annual birding festival that generates income for numerous hotels, restaurants, and other tourist facilities. The proposed project is non-invasive and will have no negative impacts on any existing cultural or historical resources.

The Refuge contributes to the economy of Northampton County by keeping land in permanent open space. This benefit was documented in a "Cost of Community Services Study(COCS)" for Northampton County, Virginia (Adams, et. al., 1999). A COCS is a case study analysis of the net fiscal impacts of different land uses. It provides a snapshot in time of costs versus revenues based on current land use. These studies are based on real budgets for a specific community. The analysis shows what services private residents receive in return for the taxes they pay to their local community.

These studies have shown time and again that open space costs towns less than residential or commercial development. The reason for this is because residential, and to a lesser extent commercial development, requires certain town services such as schools, utilities, and emergency services. Although residential and commercial development increases a town's tax base, expenses

incurred by the town for increased services far outweigh the taxes generated from residential and commercial uses.

The Refuge also directly contributes to the local economy of Northampton County through "Refuge Revenue Sharing" payments. The federal government does not pay property tax on Refuge lands, but instead makes annual payments to respective counties based on a maximum of 0.75 percent of the fair market value of Refuge lands, as determined by an appraisal every five years. The actual amount distributed each year varies and is based on Congressional appropriations in a given budget year. The amount distributed also changes as new lands are acquired. The figure below depicts the amounts distributed to Northampton County between 1995 and 2002.

Table 2. Refuge Revenue Sharing payments from Eastern Shore of Virginia and Fisherman Island Refuges to Northampton County.

	Number of Acres		Total Paid to Northampton County	
	Eastern Shore of Virginia Refuge	Fisherman Island Refuge	Eastern Shore of Virginia Refuge	Fisherman Island Refuge
1995	725	1,000	$12,241	$6,995
1996	725	1,000	$16,388	$9,364
1997	745	1,000	$16,745	$9,427
1998	745	1,825	$10,583	$16,808
1999	745	1,850	$9,403	$15,650
2000	745	1,850	$8,249	$13,728
2001	745	1,850	$8,419	$14,012
2002	1,121	1,850	$11,712	$13,090

The traditional villages and towns of the area are surrounded by farm lands and water, which provide livelihood to its residents and recreation to its visitors. Recreation includes deep water fishing, crabbing and shellfishing, camping, boating, beach-going, bicycling, hunting, canoeing, kayaking, and bird watching.

The area can be considered a seasonal destination

area. Because of its location and natural amenities, tourism plays a larger role in its economy than the industry does for the state as a whole. A residential and marina community is under development, with associated recreational uses, including golf, boating and beachgoing.

We do not predict any significant adverse socioeconomic or cultural impacts. Towns will benefit from increased refuge revenue sharing payments, savings on the cost of community services, increased property values, increased watershed protection, maintenance of scenic values, and increased revenues to local businesses from refuge visitors.

We would continue to promote the six priority wildlife-dependent recreational uses of the Refuge System, including hunting, fishing, wildlife observation and photography, and environmental education and interpretation, where they are compatible with the management purposes of each refuge. The refuge currently has a hunting program, a wildlife trail system, wildlife observation sites, and environmental education stations. These would be expanded to new lands acquired. However, we would eliminate non-wildlife-dependent activities for lands that we acquire.

Refuge lands would increase protection for cultural resources in the area. Service ownership would protect known cultural sites against vandalism, and would protect as yet unidentified or undeveloped cultural sites from disturbance or destruction. Our interpretive and environmental education programs will continue to promote public understanding and appreciation of the area's rich cultural resources.

Appendix A. Parcel Maps and Table

The maps show existing refuge lands, our proposed acquisition area, and all land parcels within that area. The corresponding table lists each parcel, its tax map and parcel number, ownership, acreage, our priority and recommended method for acquisition, and county zoning designation. The information is based on Northampton County GIS Tax Data as of December 2001.

We propose to acquire either full or partial interest in land parcels by fee purchase, as available from willing sellers over time and as the availability of funding allows. We also propose to develop cooperative management agreements with the county and several state agencies, for public lands within the project area. Definitions of each table column head follow.

LPP tract number	our numerical identifier for each parcel within the proposed acquisition boundary
Tax Map	Northampton County tax map, or "insert" number
Tax Parcel ID	Northampton County tax parcel identification number
Ownership	agency, organization, company or private landowner's last name
Acres	acreage from Northampton County tax database
Priority	Priority 1: those parcels with significant (over 1 acre) tracts of existing forested and shrub migration habitat, located in the critical immediate southern tip area (from Cedar Grove south) and along the bayside shoreline (between the bayshore and Route 645) north to Plantation Creek
	Priority 2: those parcels with significant (over 1 acre) tracts of existing forested and shrub migration habitat, located along the seaside coastline (between the seaside coastline and Route 600) from Cedar Grove north to Walls Landing Creek
	Priority 3: those parcels that consist of predominantly agricultural land with no existing forest or shrub (less than an acre) and no coastal connection
	Priority 4: those relatively small parcels, generally less than 5 acres, that include collections of buildings such as residences, farm houses, barns, various tractor and equipment sheds, farm storage or processing buildings. Our intention is not to acquire residences and buildings, but to protect or restore habitat, so these parcels will be evaluated on a case-by-case basis
Acquisition Method	For lands within the proposed boundary, whether we would acquire fee title or conservation easement (see discussion in "Acquisition Method"), or if we are proposing to develop a management agreement
Zoning designation	Northampton County zoning designation for each parcel

Bibliography/References

Mabey, S.E., J. McCann, L.J. Niles, C. Bartlett, and P. Kerlinger 1993. Neotropical Migratory Songbird Coastal Corridor Study, Final Report. Virginia Department of Environmental Quality / NOAA Office of Ocean and Coastal Resource Management.

Peter, J. and S. Harper 2001. A Special Report: Flawed Law Fails the Bay. The Virginian-Pilot, July 29 Issue 251.

Peter, J. and S. Harper 2001. A Special Report, Part 2: Exceptions Rule in Local Cities. The Virginian-Pilot, July 30 Issue 252.

The Louis Berger Group, Inc. 2001. Chesapeake Bay Bridge-Tunnel Commuter Toll Impact Study: Preliminary Draft Impact Report. 100 Halsted Street, East Orange, New Jersey.

Watts, B.D. and S.E. Mabey 1994. Migratory Landbirds of the Lower Delmarva: Habitat Selection and Geographic Distribution. Virginia Department of Environmental Quality Coastal Resources Management Program.

Watts, B.D. 1999. Draft Partners-In-Flight Mid-Atlantic Coastal Plain Bird Conservation Plan. Center for Conservation Biology, College of William and Mary, Williamsburg, Virginia.

Eastern Shore of Virginia National Wildlife Refuge
Draft Land Protection Plan
Index Map
Northampton County, Virginia

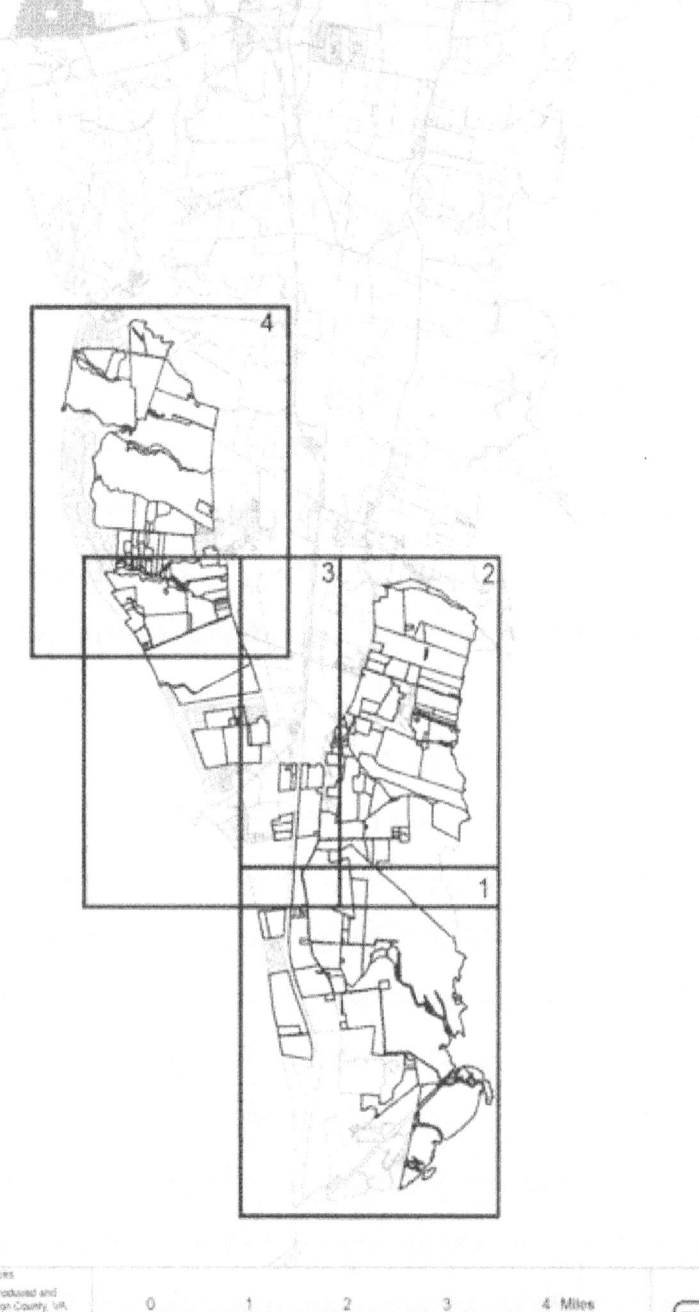

Data Sources

Digital Tax Map data produced and
provided by Northampton County, VA.
All other data provided by U.S. Fish &
Wildlife Service.

Projection/Datum:
UTM Zone 18, NAD83, Meters

Map prepared by the R5 Cartography &
Spatial Data Services Section.
March 2003
This map is for planning purposes only.

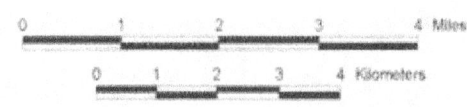

0 1 2 3 4 Miles

0 1 2 3 4 Kilometers

N

Map 1

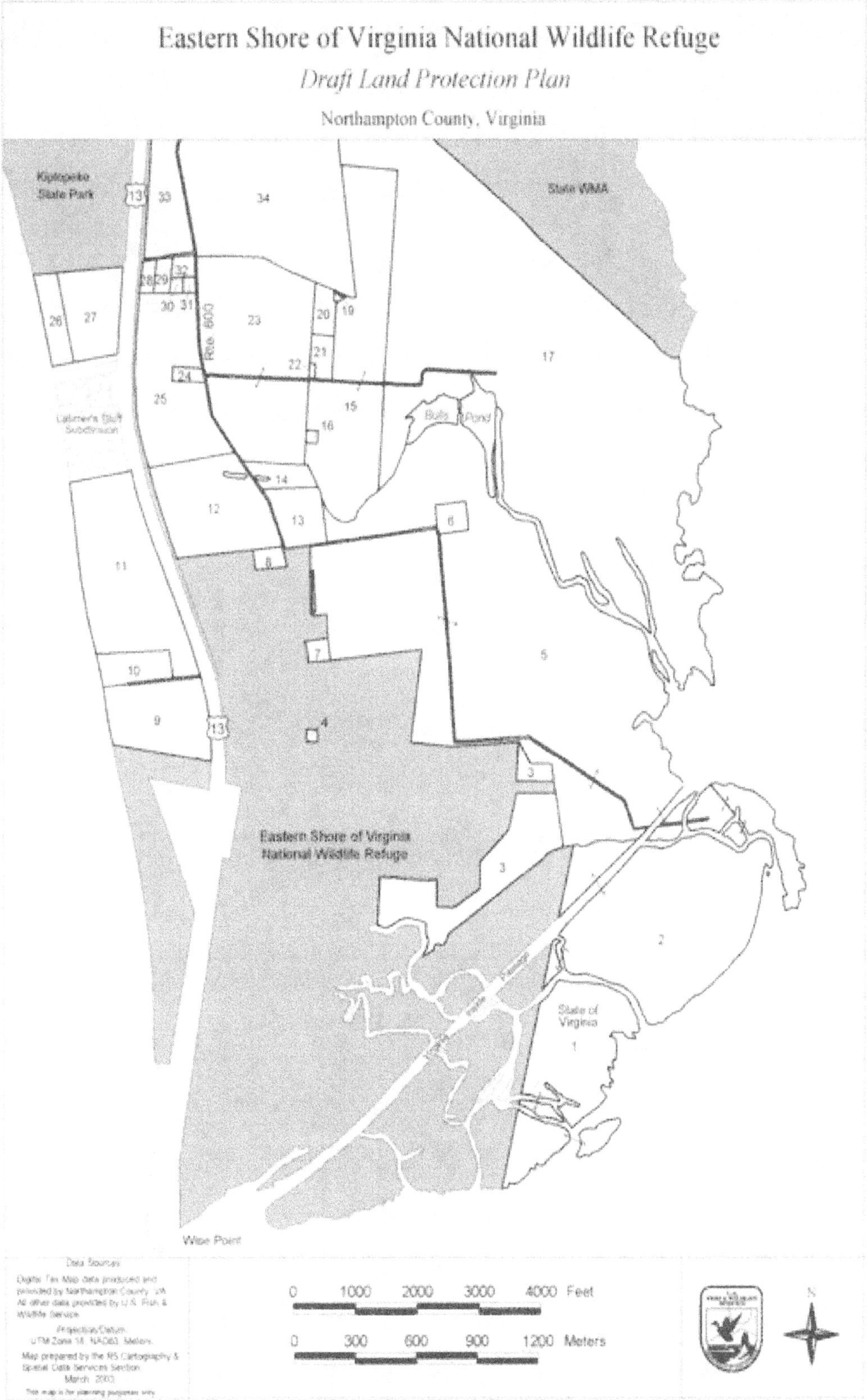

Eastern Shore of Virginia National Wildlife Refuge

Draft Land Protection Plan

Northampton County, Virginia

Kiptopeke
State Park

State WMA

33

34

28 29 32

26 27

30 31

20 19

23

22 21

17

24

15

25

16

Bulls Pond

14

12

13

6

11

8

7

5

10

9

4

3

Eastern Shore of Virginia
National Wildlife Refuge

3

State of
Virginia

2

1

Wise Point

Data Sources:

Digital Tax Map data produced and
provided by Northampton County, VA.
All other data provided by U.S. Fish &
Wildlife Service.

Projection/Datum:
UTM Zone 18, NAD83, Meters.

Map prepared by the R5 Cartography &
Spatial Data Services Section.
March 2003.

This map is for planning purposes only.

0   1000   2000   3000   4000   Feet

0   300   600   900   1200   Meters

N

Map 2

Eastern Shore of Virginia National Wildlife Refuge
Draft Land Protection Plan
Northampton County, Virginia

Map 3

Eastern Shore of Virginia National Wildlife Refuge

Draft Land Protection Plan

Northampton County, Virginia

Map 4

Eastern Shore of Virginia National Wildlife Refuge

Draft Land Protection Plan

Northampton County, Virginia

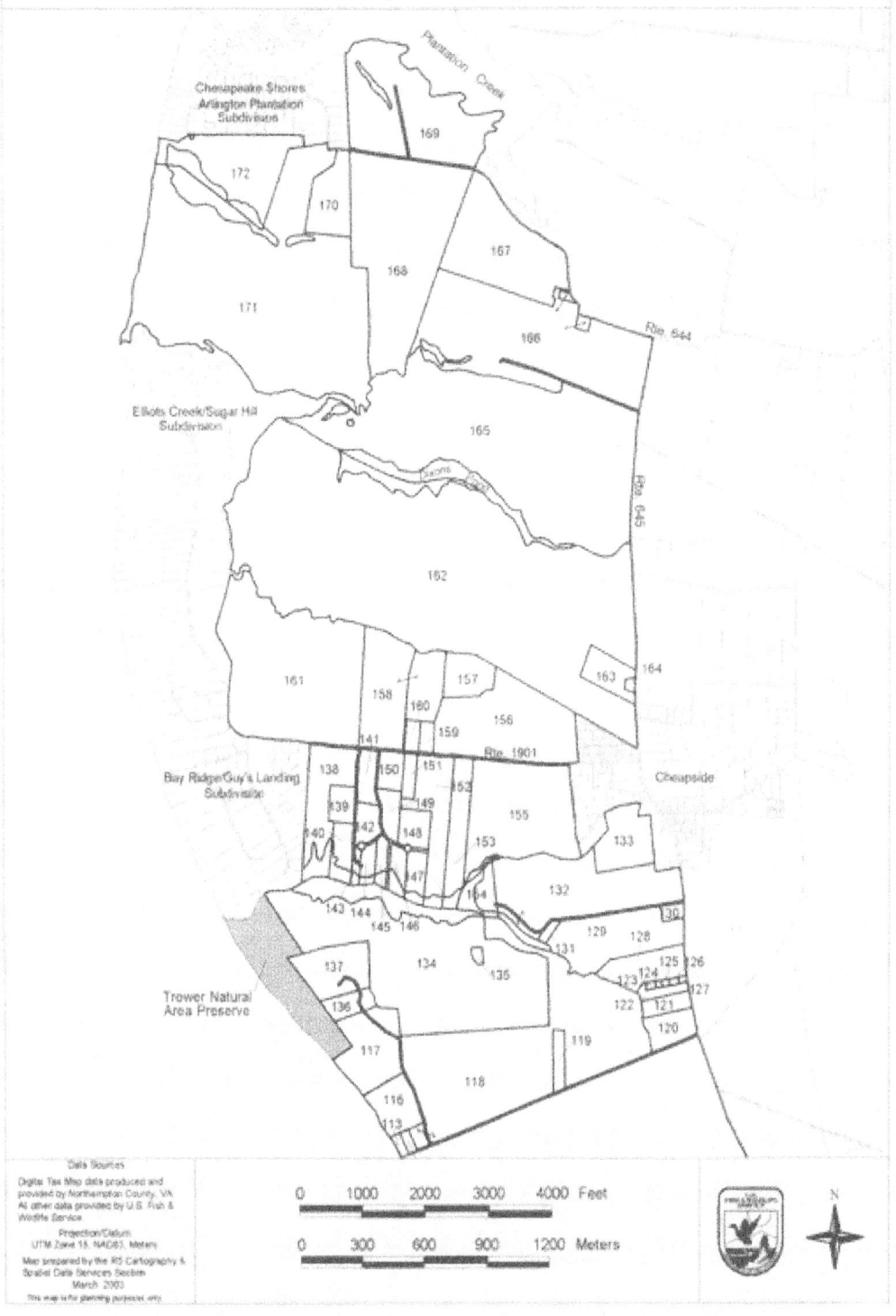

Data Sources

Digital Tax Map data produced and
provided by Northampton County, VA.
All other data provided by U.S. Fish &
Wildlife Service

Projection/Datum
UTM Zone 18, NAD83, Meters

Map prepared by the R5 Cartography &
Spatial Data Services Section
March 2003

This map is for planning purposes only.

| 0 | 1000 | 2000 | 3000 | 4000 | Feet |

| 0 | 300 | 600 | 900 | 1200 | Meters |

N

LPP NO.	TAX MAP	TAX PARCEL	LASTNAME	TOTACRES	PRIORITY	METHOD	ZONING
1	00123	003	COMMONWEALTH OF VIRGINIA	62.00	1	COOPERATIVE AGREEMENT	A
2	00123	002	HEHL L.L.C.	160.00	1	FEE or EASEMENT	A
3	00118	008	NORTHAMPTON COUNTY	10.00	1	COOPERATIVE AGREEMENT	A
3	00118	009	NORTHAMPTON COUNTY	50.49	1	COOPERATIVE AGREEMENT	A
4	00117	023	EASTERN SHORE PUBLIC SERVICE CO. OF VA.	0.91	1	FEE	A
5	00118	005	DIXON / GREGORY	380.00	1	FEE or EASEMENT	AFD
6	00118	004	DIXON	2.00	4	FEE**	A
7	00117	021	MILLER	2.11	4	FEE**	A
8	00117	020	LATIMER	2.53	4	FEE**	A
9	00117	024	SUNSET BEACH MOTEL	41.00	1	EASEMENT	EBCW
10	00117	018A	DIXON	12.05	1	FEE or EASEMENT	AFD
11	00117	017	DIXON	74.00	1	FEE or EASEMENT	AFD
12	00117	015	DIXON	46.00	1	FEE or EASEMENT	AFD
13	00117	014	DIXON	7.00	1	FEE or EASEMENT	AFD
14	00117	013	TROWER	5.00	1	FEE or EASEMENT	A
15	00118	013	LAMBERTSON	73.63	1	FEE or EASEMENT	A
16	00117	012	WILLIAMS	1.00	4	FEE**	A
17	00118	002	BULL	669.30	1	FEE or EASEMENT	AFD
19	00118	000A,B,C	VALENTINE	0.35	4	FEE**	A
20	00117	010B	EDMUNDS	5.37	3	FEE or EASEMENT*	A
21	00117	010A	EDMUNDS	5.00	3	FEE or EASEMENT*	A
22	00117	011	WELLS	0.00	4	FEE**	A
23	00117	009	SPADY	108.00	1	FEE or EASEMENT	A
24	00117	007	LATIMER	1.00	4	FEE**	A
25	00117	006	LATIMER	59.49	1	FEE or EASEMENT	A
26	00117	001	PARSONS	7.08	1	FEE or EASEMENT	A
27	00117	002	LATIMER	32.50	1	FEE or EASEMENT	A
28	00117	004	HEATH	2.03	4	FEE**	A
29	00117	006B	LATIMER	2.71	1	FEE or EASEMENT	A
30	00117	006C	SPENCER	1.04	4	FEE**	A
31	00117	006A	LATIMER	1.00	4	FEE**	A
32	00117	006D	LATIMER	3.04	1	FEE or EASEMENT	A
33	00112	109	PARSONS	55.00	3	FEE or EASEMENT*	A
34	00117	008	DICKINSON	130.00	1	FEE or EASEMENT	A
35	00112	107A	PARSONS	24.00	1	FEE or EASEMENT	A
36	00112	107B	BULL	28.23	1	FEE or EASEMENT	A
37	00113	067	JONES	8.32	3	FEE or EASEMENT*	A
39	00113	000A	LEWIS	1.00	3	FEE or EASEMENT*	A
40	00113	000B	LEWIS	1.50	3	FEE or EASEMENT*	A
41	00113	000C	LEWIS	1.50	3	FEE or EASEMENT*	A
42	00113	066	RICHARD	3.06	4	FEE**	A
43	00113	000D	LEWIS	4.44	4	FEE**	A
44	00113	064	JONES / GOODWYN	164.41	1	FEE or EASEMENT	A
45	00113	064A	JONES	0.00	3	FEE or EASEMENT*	A
46	00112	107	PARSONS	57.77	1	FEE or EASEMENT	A
47	00112	106A	GOINS	0.00	4	FEE**	RV
48	00112	106	HEATH	58.87	1	FEE or EASEMENT	RV

#	Map	Parcel	Owner	Acres	Tract	Interest	Status
49	112A2	001	COASTAL PROPERTIES-EAST INC	8.44	3	FEE or EASEMENT*	RV
50	112A2	002	COASTAL PROPERTIES-EAST INC	8.81	3	FEE or EASEMENT*	RV
51	112A2	003	COASTAL PROPERTIES-EAST INC	8.85	3	FEE or EASEMENT*	RV
52	00112	073	LATIMER	14.00	3	FEE or EASEMENT*	RV
53	00112	074	MADDOX	3.00	3	FEE or EASEMENT*	RV
54	00112	075	MEARS	2.83	3	FEE or EASEMENT*	RV
55	00112	094B	KELLAM	9.00	3	FEE or EASEMENT*	AFD
56	00112	094	SMITH	20.00	3	FEE or EASEMENT	A
57	00112	080	LYNN	12.75	1	FEE or EASEMENT	A
58	00112	091	HEATH	82.12	1	FEE or EASEMENT	A
59	00113	063	JONES / GOODWYN	16.25	1	FEE or EASEMENT	A
60	00113	061	HEATH	11.77	1	FEE or EASEMENT	A
61	00113	062	HEATH	10.83	1	FEE or EASEMENT	A
62	00113	060	HEATH	99.58	1	FEE or EASEMENT	A
63	00113	049	THE NATURE CONSERVANCY	40.00	1	FEE or EASEMENT	A
64	00113	050	THE NATURE CONSERVANCY	2.00	1	FEE or EASEMENT	A
65	00113	051	THE NATURE CONSERVANCY	0.75	1	FEE or EASEMENT	RV
66	00113	052	HEATH	100.00	1	FEE or EASEMENT	A
67	00113	059	EUDY	40.00	1	FEE or EASEMENT	A
68	00112	085	UNKNOWN	6.00	1	FEE or EASEMENT	A
69	00112	002	STILLWELL	5.00	1	FEE or EASEMENT	A
70	00112	079	AMES	5.00	1	FEE or EASEMENT	A
71	00112	078B	DANIELS	4.00	1	FEE or EASEMENT	A
72	00112	078A	JERNIGAN	4.00	1	FEE or EASEMENT	A
73	00112	032B	HARRISON	4.00	1	FEE or EASEMENT	A
74	00112	026	NOBLE / PARSONS	2.50	1	FEE or EASEMENT	RV
75	00113	058	SCOTT	16.70	3	FEE or EASEMENT*	A
76	00113	001	SCOTT	62.97	2	FEE or EASEMENT	RV
77	00113	008	HEATH	45.17	3	FEE or EASEMENT*	RV
78	00113	042	O'CONNER	21.00	2	FEE or EASEMENT	RV
79	00113	043	O'CONNER	1.00	2	FEE or EASEMENT	RV
80	00113	046	THE NATURE CONSERVANCY	0.00	2	FEE or EASEMENT	A
81	00113	042A	THE NATURE CONSERVANCY	28.19	2	FEE or EASEMENT	A
82	00113	048	THE NATURE CONSERVANCY	2.50	2	FEE or EASEMENT	A
83	00113	047	MORRIS	0.00	4	FEE**	A
84	00113	041	O'CONNER	6.00	2	FEE or EASEMENT	RV
85	00113	040	WILLIAMS	5.00	2	FEE or EASEMENT	RV
86	00113	037	VALENTINE / WILDLIFE MANAGEMENT LLP	8.16	2	FEE or EASEMENT	RV
87	00113	036	VALENTINE / WILDLIFE MANAGEMENT LLP	9.08	3	FEE or EASEMENT*	A
88	00113	035	VALENTINE / WILDLIFE MANAGEMENT LLP	45.20	2	FEE or EASEMENT	A
89	00113	033	VALENTINE / WILDLIFE MANAGEMENT LLP	25.20	2	FEE or EASEMENT	A
90	00106	086A	VALENTINE / WILDLIFE MANAGEMENT LLP	26.00	2	FEE or EASEMENT	RV
91	00106	086	VALENTINE / WILDLIFE MANAGEMENT LLP	10.00	3	FEE or EASEMENT*	RV
92	00106	087	VALENTINE / WILDLIFE MANAGEMENT LLP	23.00	2	FEE or EASEMENT	RV
93	00106	089	HAMILTON	13.00	3	FEE or EASEMENT*	RV
94	00106	000B	SCOTT	12.03	3	FEE or EASEMENT*	RV
95	00106	083	VALENTINE / WILDLIFE MANAGEMENT LLP	133.70	2	FEE or EASEMENT	RV
96	00106	071	THE NATURE CONSERVANCY	66.00	2	FEE or EASEMENT	RV

#	Parcel	ID	Name	Value	No.	Interest	Acq.
97	00106	068	VALENTINE / WILDLIFE MANAGEMENT LLP	1.99	3	FEE or EASEMENT*	RV
98	00106	067	VALENTINE / WILDLIFE MANAGEMENT LLP	5.00	3	FEE or EASEMENT*	RV
99	00106	066	VALENTINE / WILDLIFE MANAGEMENT LLP	52.00	2	FEE or EASEMENT	RV
100	00106	069	VALENTINE / WILDLIFE MANAGEMENT LLP	150.04	2	FEE or EASEMENT	RV
101	00106	070	TOWNSEND	12.00	2	FEE or EASEMENT	A
102	00112	062	DICKINSON	56.39	1	FEE or EASEMENT	RV
103	00112	063	KELLAM	64.31	3	FEE or EASEMENT*	AFD
104	00112	064	CARLISLE	3.00	3	FEE or EASEMENT*	RV
105	00112	039	SPADY	26.96	3	FEE or EASEMENT*	RV
106	00112	060	KELLAM	25.00	3	FEE or EASEMENT*	AFD
107	00112	059	AMES	3.00	3	FEE or EASEMENT*	RV
108	00112	057	AMES	1.00	3	FEE or EASEMENT*	RV
109	00112	058	ROBINSON	0.00	3	FEE or EASEMENT*	RV
110	00112	056	ROBINSON	11.00	3	FEE or EASEMENT*	RV
111	00112	001	DAVIS	84.29	1	FEE or EASEMENT	AFD
112	00105	094	MORRIS	250.26	1	FEE or EASEMENT	AFD
113	00104	015C	GOFFIGON / NOTTINGHAM	1.00	1	FEE or EASEMENT	A
114	00104	014	MORRIS	1.00	1	FEE or EASEMENT	A
116	00104	015B	NOTTINGHAM	12.14	1	FEE or EASEMENT	A
117	00104	015A	GOFFIGON	22.81	1	FEE or EASEMENT	A
118	00105	095	GOFFIGON / NOTTINGHAM	103.94	1	FEE or EASEMENT	A
119	00105	095A	HOFFMAN	3.15	4	FEE**	A
120	00105	096	MORRIS	5.00	1	FEE or EASEMENT	A
121	00105	097	MORRIS	4.24	1	FEE or EASEMENT	A
122	00105	098	PICOTT	4.24	1	FEE or EASEMENT	RV
123	0105B	005	LEWIS	0.00	3	FEE or EASEMENT*	RV
124	0105B	004	HARMON	0.00	3	FEE or EASEMENT*	RV
125	0105B	003	SESSOMS	0.00	3	FEE or EASEMENT*	RV
126	0105B	002	FITCHETT	0.00	3	FEE or EASEMENT*	RV
127	0105B	001	FAIRLEY	0.00	3	FEE or EASEMENT*	RV
128	00105	099	MOSES	10.08	1	FEE or EASEMENT	AFD
129	00105	100	YAROS	28.95	1	FEE or EASEMENT	RV
130	00105	101	SMITH	1.51	4	FEE**	RV
131	00105	100A	YAROS	1.00	4	FEE**	RV
132	00105	102	NOTTINGHAM	50.70	1	FEE or EASEMENT	RV
133	00105	103	MORRIS	14.00	1	FEE or EASEMENT	RV
134	00104	012	DETWILER	123.14	1	FEE or EASEMENT	A
135	00104	012A	NOTTINGHAM	0.81	4	FEE**	A
136	00104	015D	GOFFIGON	5.72	1	FEE or EASEMENT	A
137	00104	010	NOTTINGHAM	16.38	1	FEE or EASEMENT	A
138	00104	006B	JOYCE	23.18	1	FEE or EASEMENT	A
139	00104	006A	CAMERON	4.86	1	FEE or EASEMENT	A
140	00104	005	ELLIS	6.75	1	FEE or EASEMENT	A
141	0104C	001	GACM INC, A VIRGINIA CORP	5.00	3	FEE or EASEMENT*	A
142	0104C	002	GACM INC, A VIRGINIA CORP	5.00	1	FEE or EASEMENT	A
143	0104C	000A	GACM INC, A VIRGINIA CORP	1.43	1	FEE or EASEMENT	A
144	0104C	008	GACM INC, A VIRGINIA CORP	3.03	1	FEE or EASEMENT	A
145	0104C	007	GACM INC, A VIRGINIA CORP	1.84	1	FEE or EASEMENT	A

#	Code	Name	Sub	Acres	No.	Type	Class
146	0104C	GACM INC, A VIRGINIA CORP	006	5.02	1	FEE or EASEMENT	A
147	0104C	GACM INC, A VIRGINIA CORP	005	5.06	1	FEE or EASEMENT	A
148	0104C	GACM INC, A VIRGINIA CORP	004	5.07	1	FEE or EASEMENT	A
149	0104C	GACM INC, A VIRGINIA CORP	003	5.07	1	FEE or EASEMENT	A
150	0104C	MEAKIN	000B	5.00	3	FEE or EASEMENT*	A
151	00104	GENERAL FARMS & LAND COMPANY	003E	3.00	3	FEE or EASEMENT*	A
152	00104	LOWITZ	003D	19.54	1	FEE or EASEMENT	A
153	00104	COLLIER	003F	13.58	1	FEE or EASEMENT	A
154	00104	EDMUNDS	013	3.00	4	FEE**	RV
155	00104	GENERAL FARMS & LAND COMPANY	003A	62.88	1	FEE or EASEMENT	A
156	00104	GENERAL FARMS & LAND COMPANY	003	49.00	1	FEE or EASEMENT	A
157	00104	PRETTYMAN	004A	5.00	1	FEE or EASEMENT	A
158	00104	MANUEL FAMILY LIMITED PARTNERSHIP	004	40.75	1	FEE or EASEMENT	A
159	00104	DELSIGNORE / MOORE	003C	2.00	4	FEE**	A
160	00104	GENERAL FARMS & LAND COMPANY	003B	2.50	3	FEE or EASEMENT*	A
161	00104	WAGNER	006	91.92	1	FEE or EASEMENT	A
162	00104	DICKINSON	002	336.00	1	FEE or EASEMENT*	A
163	00105	GENERAL FARMS & LAND COMPANY	001	9.00	3	FEE or EASEMENT*	A
164	00105	INGRAM	002	1.00	4	FEE**	A
165	00097	DIXON	008	142.00	1	FEE or EASEMENT	A
166	00098	CURLING	056	86.43	1	FEE or EASEMENT	A
167	00098	STILES	059A	38.00	1	FEE or EASEMENT	A
168	00097	PARSONS	004A	85.00	1	FEE or EASEMENT	A
169	00097	PARSONS	004	65.00	1	FEE or EASEMENT	A
170	00097	BURGESS	010A	15.50	1	FEE or EASEMENT	A
171	00097	HAND	009	253.00	1	FEE or EASEMENT	A
172	00097	HAND	010	29.50	1	FEE or EASEMENT	A
173		VDCR KIPTOPEAKE STATE PARK	[535]		1	COOPERATIVE AGREEMENT	C
174		VDGIF STATE WMA - GATR TRACT	[356]		1	COOPERATIVE AGREEMENT	C
175		VDCR/HERITAGE TROWER NATURAL AREA	[35]		1	COOPERATIVE AGREEMENT	C

note: LPP numbers 18, 38, and 115 have not been used.

www.ingramcontent.com/pod-product-compliance
Lightning Source LLC
Chambersburg PA
CBHW081218280526
45787CB00006B/2439